Ancient Tools for

AWAKEN
THE ALCHEMY OF DIVINE UNION

Sarah michelle Wergin, RN, LAc

FLOWER *of* LIFE PRESS

༄

"Sarah Michelle Wergin has created a brilliant and crystal-clear guide to transformation and total well-being. Her practical, easy-to-follow steps are woven throughout with wisdom from ancient traditions. A big bonus is her clarification of the science of alchemy, called the Great Work, as she unravels the perennial mystique surrounding this art to reveal its core intention as a path of transformation into the true gold of the possible human. A great book for awakening humanity!"

—**Ani Williams,** musician, teacher, author of *Guardians of the Dragon Path*

༄

"*Awaken: The Alchemy of Divine Union* offers insights and ancient tools of transformation, turning keys of mystical awareness into a practical self-help practice. Sarah Michelle Wergin is a code-breaker bringing the ancient language of alchemy into the present. I love the way she makes the profound simple and accessible. *Awaken* is an alchemist's journey toward wholeness and ease, one we should all consider taking—not only for our own healing but that of the planet."

—**Alicia Cahalane Lewis,** author of *The Intrepid Meditator*

༄

"Sarah Michelle Wergin is a Divine Priestess, Medicine Woman, and Holistic Healer, and I highly recommend her book *Awaken: The Alchemy of Divine Union.* Sarah embodies every single word she wrote in this book—she lives and breathes this work. The ancient knowledge that she channels through this book is shared in a practical way to embody in your everyday life. Whether you long for both small and gentle daily practices or major shifts of aligning the sacred union within, Sarah weaves sacredness and wisdom to your guide into Divine Balance. Thank you, Sarah, for writing this beautiful book."

—**Amanda Sophia,** Luminary, Divine Woman Mentor, Celtic Priestess, and Feng Shui Expert, Internationalfengshuischool.com, Joinamandasophia.com, Divinewomanawakening.com

"Welcome, *Awaken: The Alchemy of Divine Union* by Sarah Michelle Wergin. Its birth into our world shimmers with hope and sweet practicality. Our favorite type of book to read is one where someone opens up their heart and their life with such boldness that we can't help but find awe and wisdom. Sarah has done that gloriously and more. She shares her story and her healing from her initiations and we are expanded beyond all reason into pure magic! Join her there. Let's all join her there."

—**Marilyn & Tohmas Twintrees,** co-authors of *Stones Alive! Vol 1-3, Grandmother Sweet Shield's Life,* and *The Rituals of Manifestation Deck and Guidebook*

"A timeless treasure! Sarah takes you on a sacred pilgrimage in every word through the depths of your soul. The words on each page not only carry teachings and guidance but an energetic blueprint of divine truth for awakening and expansion. Sarah is a trusted guide and a wealth of knowledge and wisdom. She shares it all in a way that is accessible no matter what stage of the journey you are on. This is a handbook you will reach for over and over again, each time seeing something new. I absolutely love it!"

—**Bethany Vendituoli,** LICSW

"To me, Sarah's teachings are foundational to any spiritual practice. If you are unsure where to start or where you want to take your practice, this book provides a step-by-step, spiritually pure, and defined process. Each step can be adjusted to where you want to be. My ability to comprehend more complicated efforts always comes back to what I first learned from Sarah. She has answers to the Yin and Yang of life. This book is the way to a balanced spiritual practice that gives you the flexibility to take it anywhere you need it to go. For the person with a developed practice, these are the teachings you need to elevate beyond the beyond."

—**Jamie Kingsbury,** TX

"Because we live in such difficult and challenging times, it's so important to me to have the comprehensive support and guidance available in Awaken. Using the practical recommendations to apply in my life allowed me to create a more elegant and reverent life and to thrive, not just survive. Sarah Michelle Wergin is a Renaissance woman who translates and transmits a multifaceted model of how to live so that we can flourish in a multi-dimensional life. I'm so grateful for the bounty of information in Awaken and the way I have been able to transform my life! You'll love it!"

—**Mary Guay,** LMFT, CPC, Licensed Marriage and Family Therapist, Certified Professional Coach

"Expertly weaving ancient wisdom with practical tools, *Awaken: The Alchemy of Divine Union* is a powerful guide to help you navigate your awakening in these times and emerge with authenticity and power. Sarah Wergin generously helps you to remember who you are and why you're here, assuring you that you are not alone in what may appear to be a challenging time, but is actually a potent transformation on your journey. If you want to step into your true Self with grace and strength, you'll want to turn to this book again and again!"

—**Diane Pienta,** Award-winning author of *Be the Magic*

"*Awaken* offers a treasure trove of tools and practices for establishing and maintaining awareness, self-understanding, and balance, and does so with the strength and confidence of someone with experience and wisdom. It's a handbook for enlightened freedom to be used as continued reference and inspiration."

—**Anne Reeder Heck,** author of *A Fierce Belief in Miracles* and *Float on Leaves*

"*Awaken* is an amazing resource guide of wisdom and tools to help us navigate this human experience. Filled with truth and beauty, Sarah's experience and expertise help the reader emancipate from limitation and Ascend into who and what we really are: Divine, powerful beings of light. I highly recommend this book."

—**Sally Vail,** Wealth Advisor

FLOWER of LIFE PRESS

Awaken: The Alchemy of Divine Union—Ancient Tools for Personal Empowerment

Copyright © 2024 Sarah Michelle Wergin, RN, LAc
Reach out to the author by emailing **support@awakeningdivineunion.com**

All rights reserved. No part of this book may be used or reproduced by any means, graphic, electronic, or mechanical, including photocopying, recording, taping, or by any information storage retrieval system without the written permission of the publisher except in the case of brief quotations embodied in critical articles and reviews.

Without limiting the rights under copyright reserved above, no part of this publication may be reproduced, stored in or introduced into a retrieval system, or transmitted in any form or by any means (electronic, mechanical, photocopying, recording, or otherwise), without the prior written permission of both the copyright owner and the above publisher of this book.

Because of the dynamic nature of the Internet, any web addresses or links contained in this book may have changed since publication and may no longer be valid.

Every effort has been made to ensure that the content provided herein is accurate, up-to-date, and helpful to the reader. At the time of this publishing, we make no guarantees regarding the results you will see from using the information in this book. This book is not medical advice, nor is it intended to replace medical advice. We encourage anyone to seek help from a medical professional where issues are deemed necessary. The Food and Drug Administration has not evaluated the statements contained in any information in this book. Individual results may vary. No liability is assumed. The reader is considered responsible for your choices, actions, and results undertaken after reading this work. The views expressed in this work are solely those of the author and do not necessarily reflect the views of the publisher, and the publisher hereby disclaims any responsibility for them.

Published by Flower of Life Press
www.floweroflifepress.com

Flower of Life Press books may be ordered through booksellers or by contacting:
support@floweroflifepress.com

Edited by Aimee Thunberg
Cover and Interior Design by Astara Jane Ashley
Author photo by Nicole McConville Photography, Asheville, NC

Library of Congress Control Number: Available upon request.

ISBN: 979-8-9893441-4-7

Dedication

*I dedicate this book to my Mom and Dad,
For our agreement to come into this life
and be with each other has created this.*

I love you beyond…

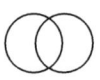

Table of Contents

A Note from the Author xiii

Prologue xvii

Illumination xix

Introduction 1

Know Thyself: Where to Start 7

Overcoming Resistance 11

Lifting The Veil 15

Your Inner Sovereign 17

Awakening Divine Union 21

What is Alchemy? 25

The Golden Thread of Truth that Transcends All 29

Midsummer Dew 38

PART 1: DISSOLUTION **39**

The Sacred Wheel of the Year 49

The Meaning of the Directions 71

Ceremony 79

Altars 85

Transcending Time 92

PART 2: PURIFICATION 93

Transformation & Transmutation 97
Detoxifying Your Body 109
Detoxifying Your Life 117
Cleansing Self & Others 135
Managing Your Energy: Grounding, Clearing, and Protection 141
The Chakra System: Basics 153
Garden 158

PART 3: REBIRTH 159

Doorway 177
Living in Divine Union 179
Conclusion 193
I AM 199
Acknowledgments 200
Resources 202
About the Author 204

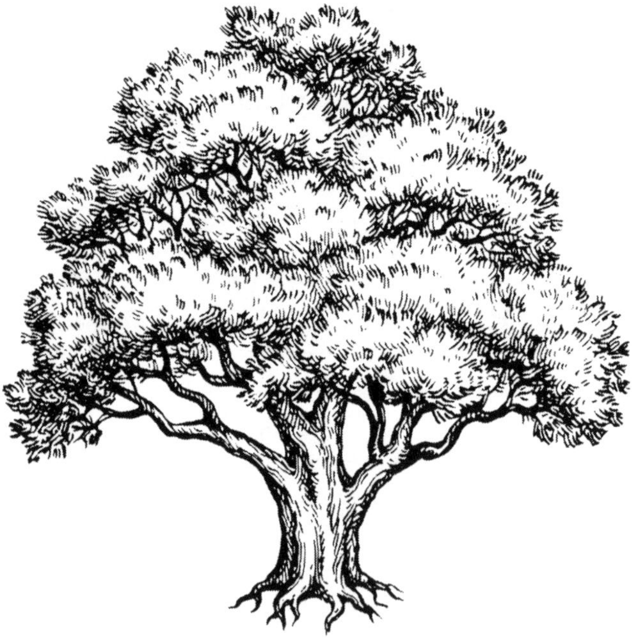

When the light shines before us, we are inspired,
When the light shines upon us, we are healed,
When the light shines within us, we are free.

—*Sarah Michelle Wergin, Aspen, CO*

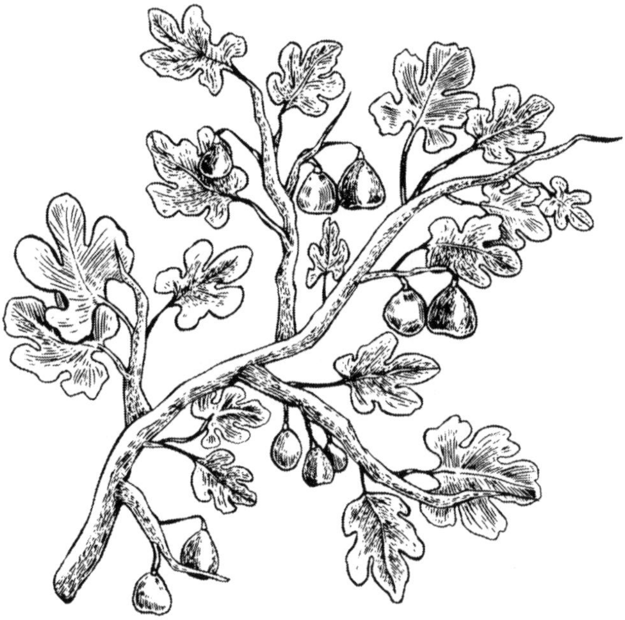

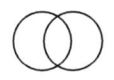

A Note from the Author

I was born a highly sensitive and intuitive child.

I would play with all of nature on our farm and loved being in the forest and among the trees and animals. At a young age, I knew there was so much more to this world than what I could see, but no one was telling me the secrets of the plants, herbs, animals, and stones.

One day, in frustration, I remember raising my arms to the sky and calling, "Show me the magic!"

I always knew my quest was to "remember" the magic that was all around me and how to use it.

I felt so much older than I looked, and I could not wait to grow up so I could actually live the life I wanted. I had an inner nagging that sounded like, "I have so much to do!"

I was born into a Catholic family and, at age nine when my parents divorced, my mother reawakened to her Goddess knowledge. I received my first crystal at 13 years old, and that began my personal quest to gather as much understanding as possible about the ancient Goddess traditions and magic.

Two weeks before my 14th birthday, I was diagnosed with cancer. At the very moment that the doctor told me and my parents, a very strange feeling came over me. It was one of joy. I knew that emotion was not what I should be feeling at that time, seeing my mother crying and my father looking so sad. So, of course, I didn't share it.

The interesting thing was, two years earlier, I had told my mother, "Mom, I cannot feel joy anymore. I see other kids around me excited for things, and I cannot feel anything." The stress of my childhood experiences had caused my energy to stagnate. It wouldn't be until later in life that I would understand this connection that led to the disease.

At that moment in the hospital room, I felt a sense of relief. I knew that, unconsciously, my Soul had created this. I knew then that my life was being forever changed, and it was a gift. I knew that my Soul had created this illness to heal me.

I soon realized that to completely heal and be healthy, I would need to understand natural healing modalities and learn as much as I could.

After recovering from my illness, I became increasingly interested in natural healing and healthy eating. I proceeded to study many different healing modalities. As soon as I trained in one, another would present itself to me. I finally opened my own integrative clinic and spent the next 30 years in the healing arts, helping others. Along this path, I also studied and practiced many different world religions and spiritualities.

Today, my spiritual path remains the most important force within me. I am here to find the golden thread of truth through them all in the quest to know thyself. I am a facilitator of light and sound, knowledge and wisdom, truth and Universal laws.

My intention is to help each person on their healing path to awaken to their true self. Only from this place can we feel wholeness and experience true healing.

I am here to support you on this journey.

You may have had years of studying and already have a spiritual practice. Or this could be a new beginning. Be wherever you are. Just take in what feels right for you at this time, and leave the rest.

Infinite Blessings,

Sarah

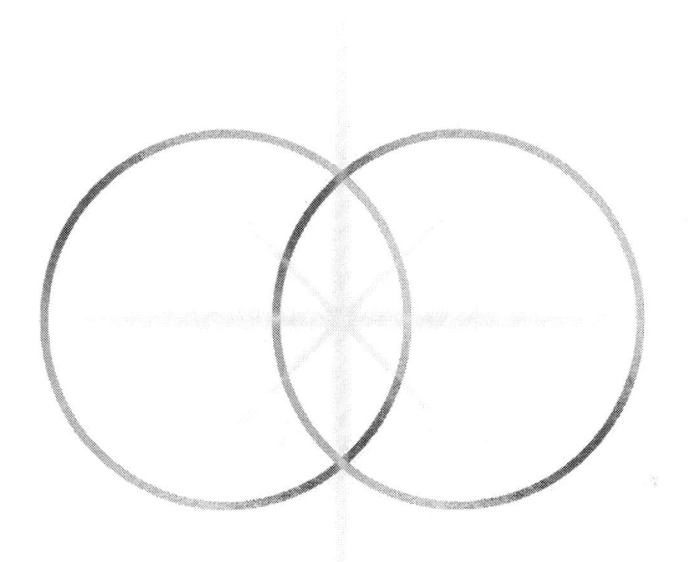

Prologue

The journey of awakening is a process of "remembrance."

We go through many lifetimes and incarnations on this planet, other celestial globes, and even other universes, all for the purpose of awakening to our knowing, piercing the veil of illusion, then stepping through it and basking in the light of Unity.

Confusion, uncertainty, pain, loss, despair, growth, elation, joy, and rebirth are all a part of the process. How long it takes, who we become, and how we travel is different for every Soul, but the truth is the same:

You are a spark of divinity embodied, a part of the ONE. And it is to the ONE that you will someday return.

As Pierre Teilhard de Chardin once wrote, discovering this truth is about remembering that you are "a spiritual being having a human experience." Many ancient traditions around the world have given us ways of remembering this eternal truth. Certain cultures, traditions, or methods will resonate with your soul more than others, but when you discover one that does, it will feel like coming home. It will feel magnetic, powerful, and comforting, and you will have a deep knowing that this is a key to open the door of truth for you.

There are many paths that can lead you to the ONE.

All are equally valid; none is more right than the others.

Your keys will find you along the way.

Having free will, you will decide if you unlock the door.

Sometimes, it just isn't the right time, and you are not ready. It can even be that someone or something around you isn't ready! When to put the key in the lock is up to you—there is no right or wrong—it all unfolds in Divine Timing.

This book is a sacred journey, a pilgrimage to your awakening. Along the way, I share ancient wisdom, channeled teachings, techniques, and experiences from the Atlantean, Lemurian, Egyptian, Buddhist, Hindu, Celtic, and Avalonian traditions.

This journey is one I offer with immeasurable love and deep knowing of how profound the information contained here can be for each Soul who is called to it.

Every pilgrimage starts with the first step. So take my hand, lovely… Onward–and inward–we go.

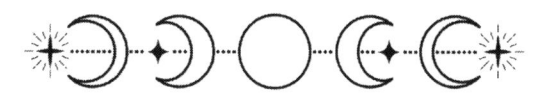

Illumination

Break open my heart, so that I may see,
What lies deep inside of me.

Too often it is hidden, what lies in the depth,
Unwilling recognition, too dark to guess.

I may hesitate to give you permission,
But in time, I will learn my mission.

It won't be kindness that I find,
Nor gentleness, nor grace,

Just the void of separation,
Leaving its trace.

In this place that lies beyond the veil,
Your truth awaits, not a fairytale.

When courage fails and you are broken in two,
You see the illumination inside of you.

Hidden on the other side of everything you hold dear,
Your armor,
Your lies,
Your illusions all clear.

Take with you only that which remains,
The knowledge of Thyself,
The only point of this game.

—Sarah Michelle Wergin

Introduction

When a Soul comes into a distinct existence as it separates from Source, it's like going on a journey. You make the plans before you depart. You leave "home" (part of Source) and go to the "train station." The train station is your journey's staging or planning area as an incarnated Soul. You decide the places you'll see and the people with whom you'll come into contact. You make agreements and a rough plan. And then you get on that train, the whistle blows, and you pull out from the station, dropping down into your incarnation.

And just like with any journey, plans get changed by what you encounter along the way—including your free will and all of the ripple effects from every other Soul. Your journey takes twists and turns, and new things happen that you never expected.

Every Soul and every life has infinite choice points to create or change course. It is at these places that our greatest growth happens.

No two Souls have the same journey. Each person is at a different point in their trajectory of awakening. The extent to which you embrace that you are a spiritual being determines the degree to which you allow Divine remembrance.

This is when you consciously begin the alchemical process.

The purpose of the many lifetimes a Soul experiences is to allow the Divine to explore the boundless possibilities of creation. Within these lifetimes, unresolved wounds are carried forward by the Soul into each subsequent existence. Through the alchemical process of birth, death, and rebirth, you have the power to transmute these areas of or denser energies into pure light.

This is why alchemy is often referred to as "The Great Work," epitomized by the concept of the "Philosopher's Stone," or the transformation of base metals into gold. Spiritual alchemy involves taking energies of a lower frequency or base nature and transmuting them into a higher frequency, akin to golden light.

Light has the power to illuminate everything, and various healing processes take place by exposing the hidden aspects of oneself and unhealed wounds to the transformative force of light. This can be achieved through acceptance and love, absorbing them into the radiance.

When I received my cancer diagnosis just two weeks before my 14th birthday, it suddenly clarified the depression, numbness, and stagnation I had been enduring for the past two years. I felt an innate understanding that overcoming cancer required a significant life change. I resolved to focus exclusively on the positive each day as much as possible while allowing myself to acknowledge and process my emotions throughout the entire journey.

Before this pivotal moment, I had been a girl with severely low self-esteem and self-confidence, often lingering in the shadows at the back of the classroom, striving to blend in and avoid drawing attention to myself. I aimed to conform and please others to ensure my safety. However, from that point onward, I made a 180-degree transformation. I began to express my true self, embracing a style that resonated with my unique personality, one that stood out and celebrated eclecticism. I also started to voice my thoughts and truth more openly.

In preparation for the hair loss I was about to experience, I decided to cut my hair short, departing from the waist-length locks I had always known. This shift in both appearance and personality resonated with a higher vibration, aligning more closely with my authentic self. It marked the necessary transformation to break free from the cycle I had been trapped in, providing my mind and body the partnership needed to combat the diagnosis. I shifted from a lower vibration to a higher frequency, transitioning from density to light.

Within us all is polarity.

Once you departed from the Source (Oneness), you underwent a division into two essential aspects of the whole: Yin and Yang. Yin embodies qualities such as coolness and darkness (darkness here refers to a state of form, moisture, inwardness, passivity, and feminine energy). At the same time, Yang represents warmth, brightness, dryness, outwardness, activity, and masculine energy. It's crucial to note that these attributes have no relation to gender and that both genders encompass elements of Yin and Yang.

In the human framework, these aspects manifest as two fundamental circuits: one characterized as magnetic (feminine) and the other as electric (masculine). These circuits give rise to various interconnected systems, perpetuating infinitely until they culminate in the creation of a human being. The presence of these two primary forces is constant within the Self.

Within the context of "Light" and "Shadow," the "Light" signifies the aspects of oneself that are healed, in harmonious flow, radiating at a high frequency, and resonating with Divine love. Conversely, the "Shadows" represent facets of your being that have incurred some form of "injury" along the way and have not healed properly. These unresolved injuries vibrate at lower frequencies, often manifesting as emotions like shame, guilt, or fear.

These fragments become "Shadows" because they are parts of you that have not received the love and acceptance they require. Left unattended, they retreat into hiding, much like a wounded child seeking to shield itself from pain. The issue is that they do not vanish; instead, they linger within the Soul until they are healed. For most individuals, these unresolved facets may resurface during times of stress or pressure.

The wonderful thing is that these Shadows are our growth points. These are where the Soul lessons are. We make this plan, agreement, or contract *before* we incarnate. In other words, you planned it!

This is your greatest mission: to find your abandoned pieces and show them you love them so unconditionally that they either come out into the light or you go in and rescue them.

You are your savior. And awakening to your truth is your mission. You are the warrior you have waited for. You have everything in you to do this.

This whole process through your lifetime—and every lifetime—is all an alchemical process. Your Soul's evolution never ends. It continues to expand, then contract, and expand again. It continues to separate or pull apart, and then recombine—over and over—purifying, transmuting, and transforming. In alchemy, it is called Solve et Coagula, "separate and recombine." This is the refining or distilling process of the purification of the Soul.

So, as you dive into the journey of awakening, realize that you are calling forth a return of all the parts of you—through all time and space. Some of these pieces will be joyful. Some will be painful. But it is all for the greater good of the whole. All of YOU belongs.

Love is ALL.

All wrongs are made right. All pain is transformed into wisdom. All evil is redeemed. All duality returns to Oneness. Love always prevails.

Knowing thyself is the key.

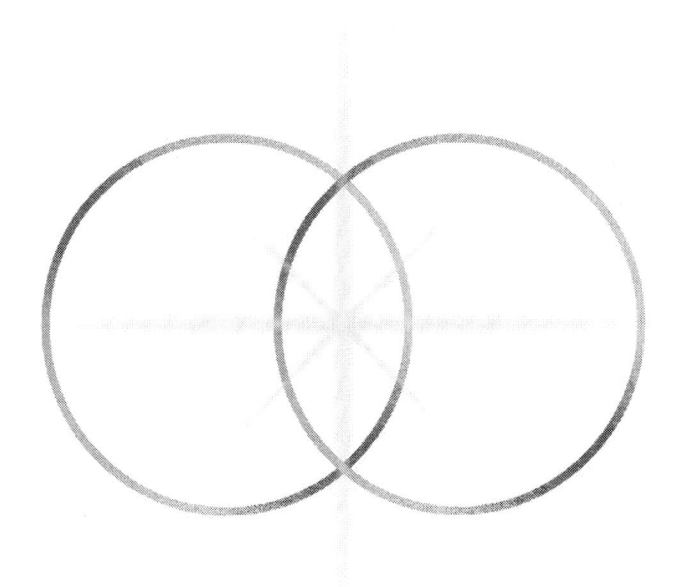

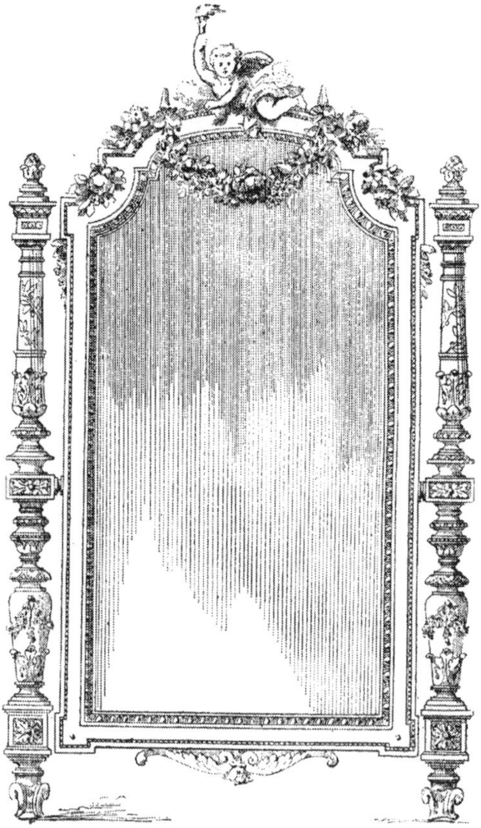

Know Thyself: Where to Start

"Know thyself."
—Temple of Apollo in Delphi

Who am I? Why am I here? What is my life's purpose? What am I meant to do while I'm here?

These questions are a part of why you have had the struggles you have had, why you have gone through your experiences, and why you face challenges.

To understand the answer to these bigger, more esoteric questions, assess your perspective of the larger themes and the smaller scenarios in these five areas:

1. Childhood

What was your childhood like? Sum up how you feel about your childhood in a couple of sentences. What were the dominant themes?

These are the areas of greatest insights into what you came to do and be. Look at your challenges, turn them around, and then see what they give you. You will see the gift and, in turn, the reason. These are important clues.

For example, if you experienced parental abuse, what emotions or traits did it instill within you? Did it foster fear, feelings of abandonment, or insecurity? Upon reflection, you'll likely recognize that you acquired certain lessons from this experience that you later used. Maybe you had to learn how to take care of yourself and discover your inner strength without having your needs met by another.

In essence, your wound may have given rise to an unfulfilled need, but it also endowed you with the valuable trait of self-reliance, which can serve as a lifelong asset. You can build upon this positive aspect of the gift while engaging in the healing process to provide your inner child with the care it needs. This transformative journey will allow you to transmute the "Shadow" aspect into the radiant "Light."

2. Relationships

What kinds of relationships have you had? Describe your relationships with your parents, siblings, friends, and lovers or spouse(s). What are the themes of your relationships?

When you go back and look at similarities through all your relationships, you will be shown the themes, which will highlight what your Soul came here to learn!

For example, if you consistently find yourself in situations where it seems like you're giving your whole self to the other person, yet the other person's affection appears to be more about what you provide than who you genuinely are, then your lesson is to embark on a journey of self-love. This involves loving yourself deeply and unconditionally for your intrinsic worth, independent of your appearance, actions, or material possessions.

3. Health

Have you had any illnesses? What were they? What parts of your body or mind have any issues? Are there recurring disharmonies?

Illness is just your body's signal to show you where the imbalances are. Every part of your body is connected to your mind, which is connected to your Soul.

For example, if you have an unhealed wound around not being heard or not speaking your truth, then your body might manifest disease in the throat area or thyroid gland. This is to get your attention! The illness starts from an energetic imbalance first before it manifests physically. Form follows energy. By the time a physical symptom appears, it has been present in the energy body for a while.

4. Patterns

There are patterns for every Soul. Reflect—objectively, compassionately—on yourself and life as if there is no wrong answer, and be honest. What patterns continue to play out in your life?

These patterns give your Soul clues about what needs your attention in order to heal and grow. Patterns can look like specific experiences or scenarios that keep showing up in your life.

For example, maybe you experience always putting so much hard work into something, and then it manifests into very little or nothing at all, and you are left feeling frustrated or hopeless. This is the Universe trying to show you that you are either doing things in a way that doesn't align with how you are created or that you need to pay attention to the essence of what you are trying to get or achieve. It is not about the thing itself.

5. Desires

What questions are you still asking yourself? What wants do you still pray for? What needs are unfulfilled?

These are areas of great revelation. Soul desires, stemming from the Divine, serve as guidance toward your purpose and mission in life. Some desires may be genuine indicators of what you are meant to do. However, there are also desires that may not authentically belong to you; they could be a result of parental expectations, family requirements, or societal standards. It is crucial to declutter and discern your own truth amidst these influences.

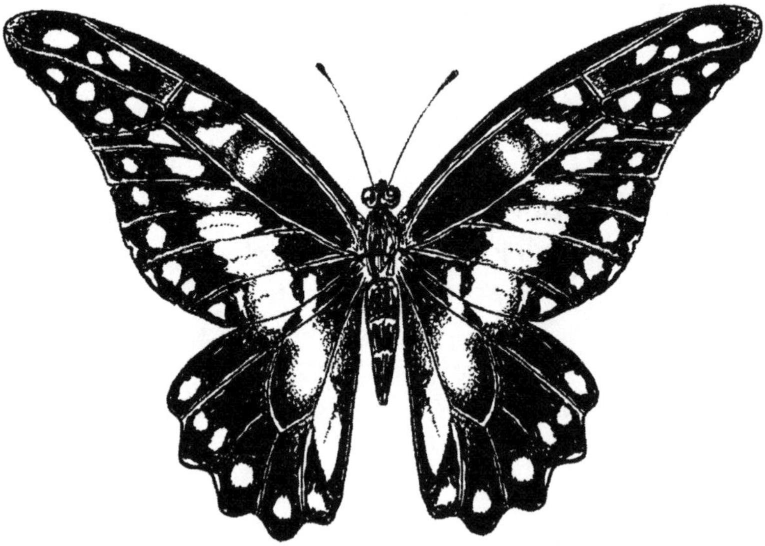

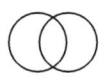

Overcoming Resistance

It is normal for you to feel a sense of uncertainty, discomfort, or even fear during life's changes. This can create resistance to what could be happening, as your Soul is shaking you or your life up to get you to pay attention.

Resistance can manifest in various ways, such as unexplained anger or heightened irritation towards things that were once tolerable. People or relationships may start pushing your buttons and triggering emotional responses. This resistance is essentially your Ego, representing your mind's attempt to maintain control for its survival. The Ego should serve as a tool directed by your Soul, not as the driving force. It operates with a limited perspective and lacks the connection to the state of Oneness.

Your Soul serves as the bridge between your Earthly personality and your Higher Self, which is linked to the Source. This Divine connection, often called "Divine Union," keeps you in the flow of love and light.

When you sense resistance to making changes in your life, even if you know change is necessary but fear the unknown or feel content with your current life, you may find that external circumstances become increasingly stressful and chaotic. These challenges are not indications that "God is not listening" or intending to harm you. Rather, they serve as the Divine's way of urging you to awaken to your highest and best good.

All your heart's true desires—your Soul and life mission—lie on the other side of you letting these things, patterns, behaviors, relationships, addictions, or lifestyles go, evolve, and change.

Resistance is like the toddler who is exhausted but doesn't want to go to bed and throws a tantrum in the process. It's that simple.

When resistance comes up inside you about what seems to be happening to you, the best thing you can do is separate yourself from people for a bit. Go somewhere and get still, get quiet, and give yourself some space. Without the influence of other people's energies, agendas, advice, opinions, or needs, you will feel a sense of opening. And in that stillness, the answers will come.

It could be in a quiet voice in your head. It could be just a knowing. It could be a feeling. It could be a sign you get.

All you need to do is suspend your judgment for a bit. Stop trying to figure it out.

Breathe and just give yourself space to not think about all the problems and things going wrong. Remember that this doesn't mean you will not have thoughts! Don't get stressed about this. Just give yourself some alone time. Let whatever comes to you come and see what happens.

The guidance needs a chance to get past the mind and drop into your heart. For the mind would only try to rationalize it, take stock of the details, figure out the "plan," run the "numbers," and do the "estimates." Sometimes, your answer, the Divine's highest path of light for you, may not make sense in that moment. DO NOT dismiss what comes. Just allow it, write it down, and sit with it.

For any change to happen, surrendering to what is presenting itself to you is the first step.

Let your heart feel some peace for a bit. Let your adrenals, your worries, and your fears all calm down. Then, you will see, know, or feel the next steps from that place.

Remember, all you need is just the next step, not the step you need tomorrow. Do not try to figure out how you are going to do something next week. The Divine works in the moment and will always lead you to the next right thing.

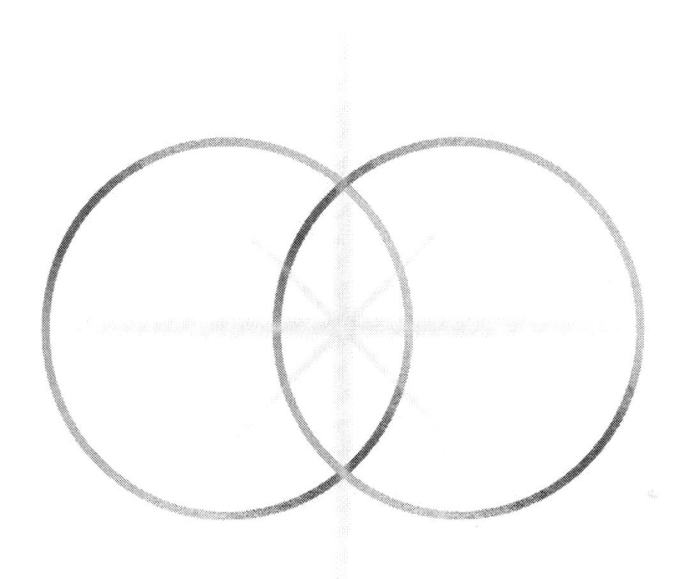

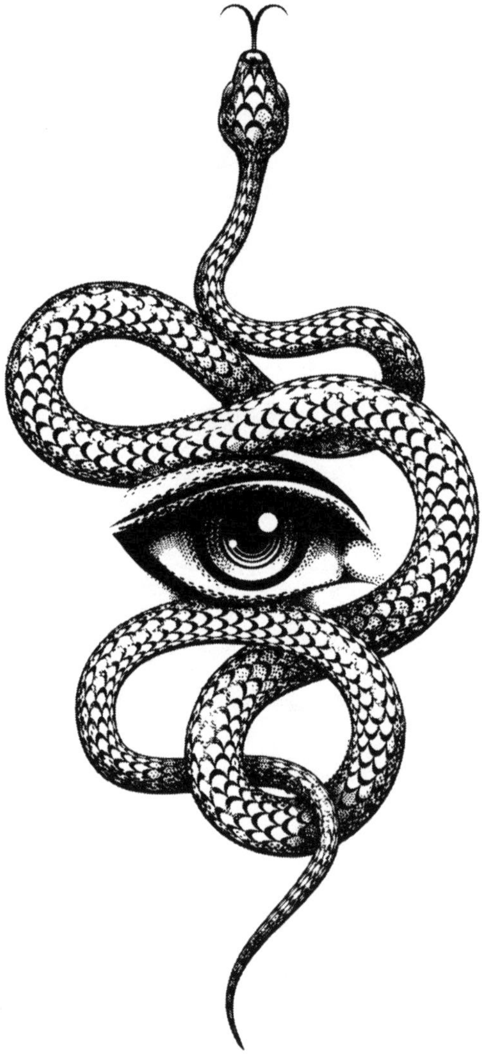

Lifting The Veil

Are you tired of repeating your past experiences and behaviors? Are you ready to move past ancestral and planetary patterns that hold you back from the joy, bliss, abundance, and prosperity meant for you?

Wake up to meet your evolved self—the Divine Union.

You can break your old patterns of thoughts, emotional expressions, and behaviors. Release all that is within you to be transformed. ALLOW it to transmute, and surrender to the process. This is how you can meet your true self.

There are those who will not see this path, who won't understand that this choice can be made. There is no right or wrong; it all belongs in the human experience on this planet. So much of what is taught, even in so-called "enlightened" circles, religious institutions, and "spiritual" teachings, are just repeated old patterns that keep the status quo/illusion/distortion in place.

It's time for a recalibration. A truly new way of BEING on Earth.

Are you ready?

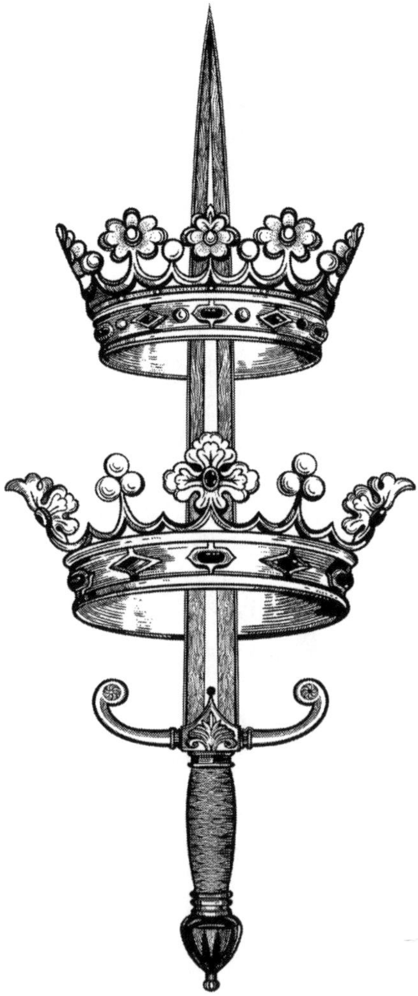

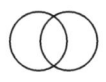

Your Inner Sovereign

"Sovereign" is the word used to define a "supreme ruler" or "ultimate power." Your "Inner Sovereign" is the concept that you are empowered and acting like the monarch of your own incarnation.

Are you?

Are you operating in your daily life with the conscious awareness that you are sitting on the throne of your reality, acting with confidence, clarity, and authority?

Or are you a servant to your own life?

The notion of co-creation and the power of manifestation, often perceived as conflicting with the mindset of being in service, should be laid to rest.

You were created by your Creator to "grow up" and become the ruler of your life!

Just as a conscious and loving parent wants nothing more than to see their child grow into their full potential and watch them expand, that is EXACTLY what your Creator is holding the space for you to do.

You were created to BECOME A CREATOR.

You are meant to become aware, confident, capable, and fully embodied. You are meant to be the one sitting on that throne of your own life and making clear choices, deciding exactly what you would like to see happen.

Every "Sovereign" has a coronation. For you, it happened when you "crowned" while being born from your mother. As a child, you had earthly parents caring for you and raising you, but they were just being the "regent" until you were ready to take the throne.

It was always YOUR throne.

As you wake up to the fact that you are royalty, take stock of your life and really see if you are acting like the Sovereign ruler that you were meant to be.

As you consider this, ask yourself:

Do I decide what I want and need to do each day—and then listen and act on it?

+ Do I think about and honor my own joy—and then make decisions on how to give that to myself?
+ Do I know my importance, worth, and value? Because without me, the whole kingdom would be in chaos…and, check yourself…is your "kingdom" in chaos? If any area of your life experience is in chaos, it is a call to you, the Sovereign, to make wise choices on what to do about it.

Being the Sovereign of your life doesn't mean that trouble and difficulty will not find you. Your life will get turned upside down many times. What it means is that even if peace in the kingdom gets disrupted by an invading power, we take stock, shore up the weaknesses, make a strategy, and then act. There will be times in life to rest, play, and fight—all while remaining sovereign.

Once you realize what this means and start to come into your Divine calling, watch how everything around you changes. People and circumstances will shift. *This is alchemy.*

"High Alchemy" is the art and science of spiritual transformation and realization. The work of a true Alchemist and every spiritual seeker is to rise above the material plane and focus on the higher ideals.

You CANNOT effectively DO High Alchemy if you are not acting like the Sovereign of your own life.

And you say… "Well, isn't the Creator supposed to be the ruler of our life? Aren't we supposed to submit to God/dess and let the Divine be in control?"

Actually, it is your small "self" or personality being in alignment with your higher or Divine Self that is meant to rule your life—your persona operating hand-in-hand with the Divinity that flows through you.

Your Creator can bring all the things before you, but if you don't know your heart and Soul, if you don't open your hands to them and take action, NOTHING is achieved.

Just as the Divine is the one who ordains the Monarch, your Creator has ordained you to lead your life. It is time to take your throne, own your power, and ascend.

You are made with Divinity within you. You are the one who can give you what you seek.

You are the one you have been waiting for.

You are precious.

You are Divine.

SOLVE ET COAGULA

Awakening Divine Union

Awakening Divine Union is precisely what the ancient ones—the sages, mystics, prophets, and priestesses—have taught since the beginning of time: the true integration and union of the masculine and feminine energies within ourselves and Source.

Awakening Divine Union, as I teach it, is the process by which an individual remembers how to reconnect to the Divine Self that is within and live as an empowered being, knowing how to use one's inner guidance, strengths, gifts, and personal tools to live their mission and purpose here in this lifetime.

It is about your connection but also your activation.

Everyone has a connection to the Divine, or Source, from whence they came. At birth, it is the Source of Creation that merged with a Soul, looking out of the eyes of the newborn. As we go through life and age, depending on our environment, we lose the remembrance of that connection. We also go through many situations, experiences, and circumstances that condition us, creating a "dis-connection" or "veiling" process. Everyone experiences a different level of this. The process of Awakening assists in a recall of the connection. Clearing the "old" learned behaviors and conditioning can assist this reconnection.

The activation is a little different. One can use tools, exercises, and initiations to reignite dormant pathways to assist the Awakening process. This is done with care only when the person is ready. It is paramount that activation goes at a pace in line with the readiness of the Soul. This is why studying or working with a teacher/healer of integrity is important.

Awakening Divine Union is about one's connection to Source—an open, fluid, and innate connection that is available to anyone. It is also about a person living their life "in tune" with their inner guidance, which comes from a higher place.

The Awakened Self—Divine Union—is everyone's birthright.

With this union, you will align and from that point, start the real journey of living as your expanded Self. You will be the Living Light, and that serves many purposes. The biggest gift is that you will be liberated. And by being so, you will help liberate others.

Take time at these different stages in the journey. Bask in your accomplishments. This is NOT a race. The rewards are the moments of bliss, joy, happiness, peace, and serenity that you receive. Take time to really feel them and give thanks. The next mountain will come. You don't need to run to it. Have fun, enjoy, play, rest, rejuvenate, share, receive. BE. Each time, you will get better at dancing up the mountain instead of schlepping.

There is no perfect way to go up that mountain!

Some people will put a smile on and try not to let the pain show through their perfect hair and ironed shirts. Some people will sweat and grunt, spewing curse words under their breath the whole way and not even look up. Some people will fall to the side of the trail, flat on their back and cry. Some people will stop every few steps and look around, taking in the view. Some people will twist their ankle or break their leg and retreat back to camp…more than once on the journey up that mountain.

The human experience encompasses a vast array of phenomena, and each one is valid.

So, why embark on this journey instead of staying comfortably asleep, nestled under the covers? The answer lies in the transformative power of a glimpse, a moment of insight, or a hint of knowledge. Once you've had a taste of the unknown, the curiosity becomes insatiable.

The allure of material pursuits eventually loses its grip when it fails to fulfill your deeper yearnings. This realization sparks the quest for wisdom as you seek meaning beyond the confines of the material world.

Every transformation you undergo, every wound you heal, each forgiveness extended, and every act comprehended sends ripples across the ocean of Souls. These ripples reach the shores of another person's island, prompting them to pause and reflect, creating an opening for awakening.

We are all in this together, and *no one* is disposable. So, hold space in yourself with the greatest and deepest patience and tenderness you can feel. And then extend that to the person next to you, for you are both the same.

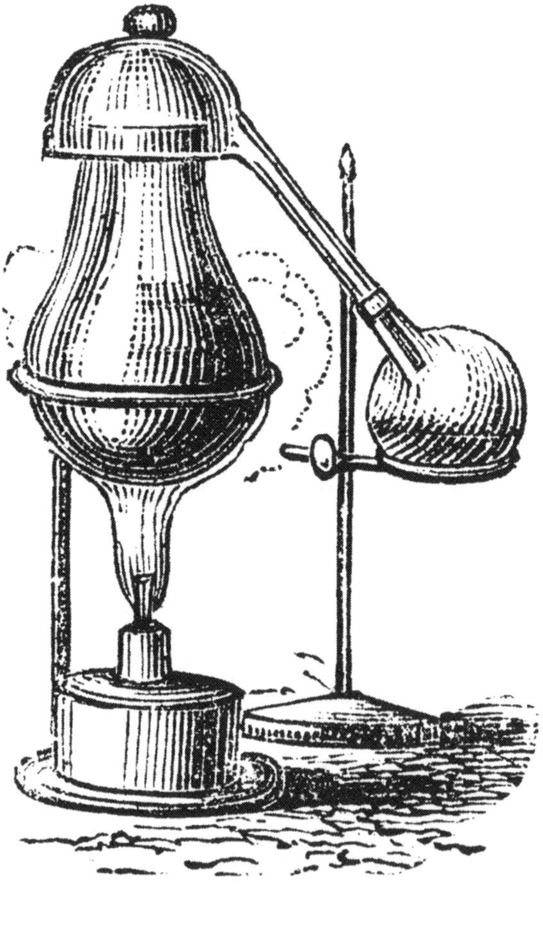

What is Alchemy?

While commonly associated with the literal transformation of base metals into gold, high alchemy also describes the internal process of spiritual ascension.

It is the process happening within you to turn your density (the unprocessed or repressed emotions) into light, merging earth and heaven within you, melding the Divine Masculine and Divine Feminine within you. In Tibetan culture, this integration is called "Ground Luminosity" or "the mind of the clear light."

In Tantra, the focus is on directing the red and white energies through the central column, aka the spine. "Red" is identified with the female essence and represents the seed of wisdom. The "white" is the male essence and represents the seed of compassion. This is the elixir of ecstatic joy.

To achieve this final blissful integration of opposites requires the death of all that has gone before.

The red and white substances are repeatedly separated and reunited, as seen in ancient images across cultures of the serpent or dragon eating its own tail.

These red and white energies correspond to the two circuits that humans carry. One is a magnetic circuit, Yin, feminine in nature, and the other is an electrical circuit, Yang, masculine in nature. The feminine principle relates to FORM, while the masculine principle relates to ENERGY.

Depending on how you look at these energies, "Red" can also be associated with heat. It congeals or fixes a form. "White" can be identified with cold and wateriness that dissolves form. These two substances repeatedly combine and separate.

In the alchemical process of spiritual awakening, the physical substance—the Soul or light body—is transmuted through a spectrum of colors: from black to violet and then to red. There is heating and form, and then watery dissolution and cleansing once again. Repeated over and over, preparing to receive illuminous spirit, the vapor rises and then descends to create the white powder, stone, or elixir. This is the feminine principle.

The "red" substance imposes form on the formless "white" stone through its heating process and turns the "white" to a "red" powder in a permanent change of color, representing the embodiment or fixation of spirit.

In Eastern traditions, it is said, "Form is Emptiness, Emptiness is Form." In alchemical terms, these primary ingredients are alternately heated, cooled, and then sealed in an alembic container.

This process represents the deepest spiritual transformation: the reborn and rebalanced Divine Masculine (God) energy that complements and conjoins with the Divine Feminine (Goddess) energy. The union of the Solar King with that of the Lunar Queen. This elevated state—Divine Union—is personal and collective.

To describe these stages, I will use the Latin/Sanskrit names that address the Black, White, and Red stages of the alchemical process. These are the forces of creation.

In short, this ever-repeating process looks and feels like this:

1. **The Black Phase (Nigredo/Tamas), aka "Dissolution"**—The alchemical process begins with the symbolic death, a painful descent into the underworld-like chaos of unformed matter. It corresponds with a major crisis. A frustration of life-changing direction and may even have an accompanying depression.

2. **The White Phase (Albedo/Sattva), aka "Purification"**—This is a process of washing or purifying to begin the release of the spirit or of a new life cleansed of the past. Loss of form is repeated as you begin to work with your inner and outer polarities.

3. **The Red Phase (Rubedo/Rajas), aka "Rebirth"**—This phase brings the emergence of a reborn and rebalanced Divine Masculine/Feminine energy.

This is the alchemy that takes place within your body. The red and white serpents or dragons spiral up your spine and merge to create potent "elixirs" that transform everything in your life. This process can take months or years, depending on your process, your willingness to surrender, and your acceptance.

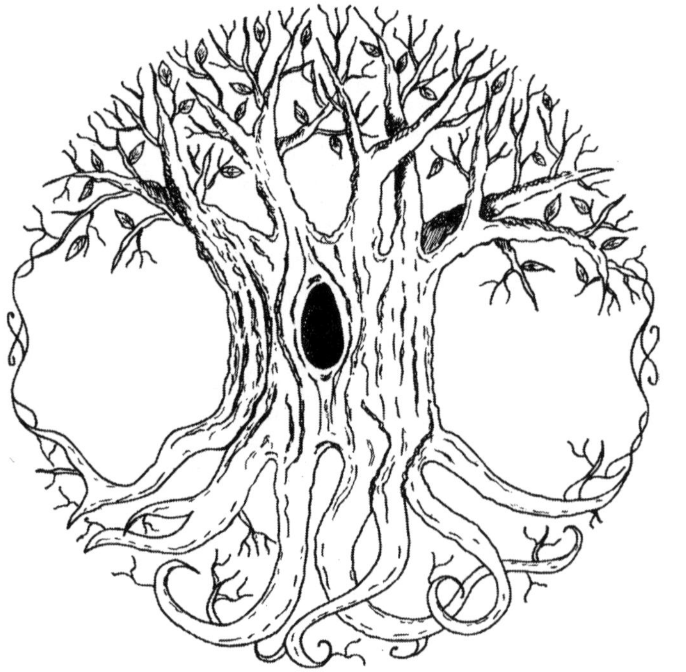

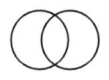

The Golden Thread of Truth That Transcends All

These phases of spiritual alchemy also correspond to three fundamental forces of nature. In Sanskrit, these are known as "gunas"—Tamas, Sattva, and Rajas. In the Western Hermetic and Magical Kabbalah traditions using Latin, they are known as Nigredo, Albedo, and Rubedo. They are inherent in every living thing, including (and most especially) your human experience.

There are stages, and, of course, there are always stages within stages. But, having awareness or consciousness of these processes can be beneficial. It can bring a sense of understanding, and from that place, knowledge and wisdom can grow. But remember, it's important not to attach even to these pieces of understanding and information. They are catalysts—not absolutes—eventually merging into One, when Divine Union occurs.

The Nigredo/Tamas stage (Dissolution) represents darkness and chaos.

In the Taoist tradition, it is the Yin: the negative, feminine, earthly, downward, receptive energy. If Albedo/Sattva is light and white, then Nigredo/Tamas is dark and black.

Nigredo/Tamas is responsible for wisdom and intuition, the inward direction of consciousness that is necessary for personal growth and development of consciousness. This stage in the Hindu tradition relates to the god Shiva, the destroyer of ignorance. Destruction and dissolution are absolutely necessary for any new growth. In the Christian tradition, Nigredo/Tamas is represented by the Christ or Christos aspect of the Trinity, for that is what destroys ignorance and replaces it with pure unconditional love and bliss.

Nigredo/Tamas is more of that inward energy that can be very intense. Wisdom is not light and fluffy but much more substantial. This state is maximal in its highest degree of enlightenment—Unity—because all duality has been destroyed.

Nigredo/Tamas can feel like unhappiness, depression, and disease because it's what is destroying ignorance of all things on an earthly plane. But, in the highest stage of consciousness or enlightenment in Unity consciousness, all perception of duality is destroyed, and thus, it is elevated. But it can feel very dense or intense.

This is a nuance to meditate upon.

When you are in the stage of Nigredo/Tamas, it can feel like things are falling apart in your life; things are not going "right." This is because many people associate their daily activities with being so important, real, and critical to their survival. What begins to happen is that any distortions in life keeping you from understanding your true self, life mission, or highest good will begin to break apart, which can look like loss and may feel very painful. There seems to be a lot of conflict, heaviness, and sadness. When we take our awareness above the earthly plane to higher consciousness, what is truly happening is the dissolution of ignorance. The facade of the illusion starts to crumble. Transmutation is happening in this stage, and it can be precarious.

When you are still in Nigredo/Tamas, you can be moving a lot of energy. At this stage, there can be the temptation to numb the pain.

In the absence of adequate guidance, when the Soul hasn't attained a level of awakening to grasp its mysteries and tools, or when it loses hope and withdraws, turning to elements that deepen its state of darkness, a window opens for non-benevolent negative energies in the universe to infiltrate and take control.

That mental state can allow for doubt to come in, leading to confusion and fear. That is an opening. A person or a Soul can end up dwelling here too long without doing the work and end up getting lost.

Many people will try and use things to numb out, ignore the process, or stop the process altogether. That will also delay evolution. The quickest way through it is to go into it completely and fully, allowing the self to experience whatever is showing up, no matter how painful.

But many Souls will self-medicate with substances, foods, environments, or people that match the perceived truth of where they're at. Ignorance of what is actually happening can take the person into lower and lower frequencies and hold them there, not really doing the transmutation work. And that has the potential for destruction.

If the person is able to do the work of transforming and transmuting, then this is where the illumination will light the darkness and purify the density.

Sarah's Dissolution Story

I had created a thriving and profitable holistic healing clinic and was so fulfilled. I had manifested exactly what I had envisioned and was very happy. I also met a new love and got engaged to be married.

As we were deciding where we would live, as he was working and living in a town three hours from me, I began to struggle with my choice. Should I close my clinic in this location and risk starting over in a whole new community, having to build a practice from the ground up again? Or stay where I was and keep building on the hard-earned success I had made?

Over time, my practice began to slow down, appointments dwindled, and I began to sense that something needed to change. I grew more and more worried about my practice and was experiencing fear about what was happening to everything I had built.

I eventually realized that the life I had passionately crafted, investing my heart and soul, was reaching its natural conclusion. The notion that this was the final vision for the rest of my life proved terrifying and confusing. Yet, understanding the need to let go, express gratitude for my achievements, and embrace a new path, I made the decision to sell my practice and belongings. I committed to moving to my fiance's town, embarking on a journey to rebuild my practice and life.

The move to the new town not only brought prosperity to my practice but also enabled me to purchase my dream home. Additionally, a lifelong childhood dream of owning a horse became a reality. Allowing the dissolution of my old life led to even greater fulfillment of my dreams.

The Albedo/Sattva stage (Purification) is the "white" stage known as absolute purity.

Albedo/Sattva is the maximal in the exalted consciousness. It is a state of balance, harmony, and peace. In the Christian tradition, the Albedo/Sattva power is represented by the Holy Spirit. In the Taoist tradition, it is the Yang: positive, male, expansive, heavenly, or upward energy.

The Albedo/Sattva stage is the illumination. There is a sense of purity and peace: a clean slate, an opening of awareness. You can see and understand things clearly. This can result from exiting a Nigredo/Tamas phase where a lot of transmutation and purification have taken place. What is important to understand about this stage is that, as with all stages, it is not the end. It's just another experience.

At this stage, there is a deep sense of "connected unity." This understanding can bring great relief. You reflect, see where your attachments have been, and have unconditional love for the whole experience.

It's common to declutter your body or environment during this phase—if you haven't already. This will be a purging energy, as well. Letting go of what is old, stuck, or dense will feel good and create spaciousness. You will want to make changes. What you prefer to eat or drink, or the people you prefer to be around, could change. People can drop out of your life. Relationships can change or end. It's important to remember that none of these people or relationships were "bad." They are just no longer a vibrational match for you.

You may also have inspiration and guidance to change big aspects of your life, like your lifestyle, personal choices, career, relationship status, and where you live.

This stage can feel light! And you will want to lighten up your life, as well.

Sarah's Purification Story

At the age of 13, I received profound inner guidance urging me to clean up my diet and embrace healthier eating habits. It's crucial to note that this was 35 years ago when there were no large natural foods stores. Although small and tucked away, co-ops were the go-to places for "healthy" foods. When I expressed my desire to become a vegetarian to my family, they were perplexed, considering our usual diet of macaroni and cheese, hot dogs, canned chow mein, and processed soups and vegetables. Nevertheless, this inner calling sparked my exploration into incorporating more vegetables and adopting a healthier diet, which became a newfound passion.

Little did I know that a few months later, I would be diagnosed with cancer, and the dietary changes I had initiated would play a pivotal role in my fight against it. My body and soul were communicating with me!

(On a side note, since then, I have pursued and become certified in various holistic healing modalities, including blood typing, genotyping, Chinese Medicine, and Functional Medicine, among others. Today, I acknowledge and understand the importance of dietary choices based on individual principles; animal products are not inherently bad, and it depends on the circumstances. However, at that time, the shift to vegetarianism was perfect for me, guiding me towards consuming more whole vegetables and cleaner animal products while reducing processed foods.)

The Rubedo/Rajas stage (Rebirth) is the connecting link between Albedo/Sattva and Nigredo/Tamas.

Where Albedo/Sattva and Nigredo/Tamas are always working together, Rubedo/Rajas is the bridge. It represents activity and passion.

It is like the infinite bridge between pure creation and pure destruction. It is the governor of energy. It is neutral in direction. Rubedo/Rajas is responsible for the waking state, dominating perpetual consciousness. So, as the outer world continues, the inner reality shifts the perception of Source. In the Christian tradition, it is the God/Father energy. In the Taoist tradition, it is represented by the Yin within the Yang, and the Yang within the Yin.

An imbalance of Rubedo/Rajas can be excitability, anger, or violence because of its fiery, passionate nature. While Rubedo/Rajas is dominant in perpetual consciousness, silence is the means to the more refined states of enlightenment.

The mundane human world is really Rubedo/Rajas in nature, this tension between destruction and peace.

This stage can feel like being super blissed-out, exalted, very bubbly, with lots of outward action, and passionate—positive or negative, depending on quality, direction, and amount. It's really about balance. When one is in this stage and it's balanced, it can be very blissful. There can be a lot of energy and direction happening, or creation happening, as well. It can be similar to what Albedo/Sattva feels like, except that Albedo/Sattva will be calmer, more stable, and more peaceful. Rubedo/Rajas is more exuberant.

Remember: these stages are not absolute.

These are forces of creation. They flow in and out of each other. They always have one in the other. And one doesn't necessarily precede the other. Really, there is no beginning and no end. It can look like a stepping-stone process. From perpetual to exalted to unity. Perception is always shifting and becoming more refined if one is on a dedicated path.

When we apply this understanding to our alchemical process—our evolutionary experience—it is beneficial to reflect on where we are and simply observe with no attachment. Just witness what is happening.

Being in observation carries no judgment. All is beautiful, divinely timed, and coming from a place of love as we journey back to Source. The awareness is supportive and helpful.

Even if you are in excruciating emotional, physical, or spiritual pain and agony going through a Nigredo/Tamas phase, you can still be in perpetual and conscious observation. There are parts of you that haven't been fully integrated, and it can feel like they are dying as you let go of them. As you rise up to the next level of consciousness, Nigredo/Tamas has to come in and destroy whatever ignorance resides at that level so that you can go on to the next.

Sarah's Rebirth Story

After more than a decade of running a holistic healing practice, I started to feel a growing internal dissatisfaction. While I cherished my healing practice and its components, a profound desire to elevate my Priesthood practice to a central focus in my life became increasingly powerful. The urge to dedicate all my time to receiving, sharing, and teaching the messages intensified. However, the question lingered: How could I make a living while pursuing this passion? Delving into daily ceremonies, I explored this inner voice and calling, navigating through tears and fear, journaling the emerging ideas, and sketching out the outlines of a "dream" life in my big sketchbook.

Maintaining gratitude for my clinical practice, I allowed the creation of what the next phase might look like. Taking a courageous leap of faith, I ultimately closed my clinical doors, continuing to treat friends and family while channeling all my energy, vision, and passion into creating a Mystery School based on years of channelings and teachings. Guided to take it online and establish a brand, the setup proved fortuitous when the Covid Pandemic hit. I found myself well-prepared for the widespread shutdown, my work and offerings proving more necessary than ever. The Divine guidance embedded in those Rebirth whispers turned out to be unexpectedly crucial during a time I could not have foreseen.

Why is any of this valuable to understand?

The overview of spiritual alchemy helps us understand that nothing ever stays the same. There is no static situation. Everything is changeable. Everything is a process. Even when you reach another state of enlightenment, that does not stay the same. There are ever-more refined stages within that stage. It's just a nuance that can become more and more subtle from the outside, possibly to others. But on the inside or inward reality, a lot is going on.

Because your perception—your consciousness—becomes ever more great, expansive, universal, cosmic, or all-knowing with every new understanding and added wisdom, there opens another universe of experience and reality that then expands infinitely.

Creation is never-ending because there are infinite possibilities to experience. And that is what you are: infinite possibilities. Sink into your wisdom and actively use your understanding. At the same time, learn how to be receptive and surrender.

Doing both simultaneously—being active and also in surrender—is the key.

Surrender is an act of opening. By stopping the "trying" and "holding on," you shift into magnetism. Then you are pulling towards you without effort—you are "allowing." And in that state, we can be attracting and in surrender at the same time. *It is the difference between receiving and taking.* In both instances, you "get" something, but in completely different ways.

In the alchemical process, whatever stage you are in, BE in it. Observe. Release the fight against it. Resistance is futile.

Surrender and allow. Magnetize to yourself that which is meant to come to you. It will allow for rest, rejuvenation, and also clarity because your mind won't be controlling you. Allow all thoughts to be okay and just see them absorb into the light. Just let it all come, whether that be for minutes or days. And watch without attachment to any of it lasting forever or even being true. Truth will be what shows up once all is still.

This is the magical elixir that will transform your existence. This is pure alchemy.

Let's talk about the different stages of alchemical transformation in more practical terms and the ancient tools that can help you navigate it, increasing your power as the sovereign of your life.

Midsummer Dew

At dusk and dawn, the veil is thin,
Do not despair, go within.

Not so much thought or doubt,
You are never forgotten within or without.

Befriend the dream of what your heart does seek,
In a cloud of rapture, enveloping the meek.

It sings to you through your doubt and Shadow,
Always knowing beyond knowledge what your Soul does ask for.

Too close to feel, so you feel you are lost,
Do not forsake my child, there is wisdom beyond cause.

Open your hand and it shall reach for you,
Dripping down the vine like enchanted midsummer dew.

Your heart will open and be ripped with pain,
Do not look behind,
Forever changed,

Never the same.

—Sarah Michelle Wergin

Part 1: Dissolution

Who we are now is always dying to who we are becoming.

From a spiritual perspective, this describes the refining process you experience as you evolve on your spiritual path.

This first stage, also known as Nigredo/Tamas, is where the self has to die or be dissolved. In this stage, you face your Shadow side, your wounds, or your "demons." It is the conquering of the inner dragon (or dragons). And this phase is sometimes called having a "Dark Night of the Soul."

For many people, this stage is preceded by something that happens where there starts to become a heaviness, state of frustration, depression, or some other lower-vibration emotion that begins to infuse daily life. It shows up as having a hard time enjoying life in some way or reaching a place where you can no longer ignore the inner feelings that are overwhelming you regularly, or a painful or challenging event that happens to you.

The feelings can be anger, dissatisfaction, frustration, anxiety, depression, melancholy, not being able to feel joy, excess worry, or any type of deep dissatisfaction in your life.

These emotions are intended to be catalysts, telling you something is out of balance.

Illness can come along with this—or even be the cause—because the physical body will manifest what is energetically present. Our bodies give us signs when something is wrong. And it is meant to be a signal to take the time and see what needs your attention. Where in your life or energy body (mental, emotional, or spiritual) is there an imbalance that needs to be addressed?

It could also show up as a tragic event or relationship falling apart, a career that no longer fulfills you, a child who is struggling, a crisis within a family, or an addiction that comes to a critical level. It can show up in so many ways.

Whenever a situation within yourself or your life is creating stress or chaos, look deeply. What is it trying to tell you?

If you listen closely, you will hear your Soul saying, "It is time for dissolution." Something needs to be destroyed, changed, extinguished, vanquished, transformed. There is something NEW that is asking to be born.

The extent to which you ignore this call will be the extent to which you suffer.

All suffering is attachment. Surrendering means allowing your emotional and mental attachment to be released. Allow for the change and integrate it in as if you are opening your arms with unconditional love to the whole experience and welcoming it in all its difficult realizations, complex feelings, confusing signals, misunderstood patterns, and burdened ideals.

When you welcome in the ending, you are holding sacred space for your own process.

It may be grief, sadness, or anger—let it express itself, just like a child may need to have a tantrum. When it has exhausted and released the frequency of what was being carried, it is transformed into a state of acceptance…then peace…and then there is space for the excitement of the new experience that is to come.

Nothing ever leaves your experience unless something better is coming.

Pain is our human experience because we FEEL. The secret with pain is to be grateful for whatever we are feeling—WHILE WE ARE FEELING IT, the sorrow and the joy—not only because we know that this "too shall pass," but because getting to experience it at all means we are alive!

It is a gift to feel! It is why we choose to be human in the first place. For not all life forms can feel like we do. Feelings are also our tools, guiding us to shift, expand, and evolve.

Emotions are the catalysts that move us in a direction, whether that be internal or external. They are tools and signposts to help us navigate where to focus our attention next.

When we have exhausted all our usual ideas, methods, coping mechanisms, and beliefs, we usually cry out for help—and that cry will be heard, though it is not always the answer one wants to hear. But there is an answer. Always.

Case Study: Andrea

One of my clients, Andrea, fell victim to identity theft when she unwittingly disclosed her password to a scammer, resulting in a substantial drain on her savings. As a single mom working for a non-profit, the financial blow left her uncertain about meeting her mortgage obligations. Overwhelmed by fear and anxiety, Andrea also battled a severe case of poison ivy that engulfed her entire body, subjecting her to both emotional and physical agony simultaneously.

Raised with a strong sense of independence, Andrea's initial response was to reach out and seek my assistance, a gesture she hadn't easily embraced before. When I suggested that her soul might have orchestrated this ordeal as an initiation, she began to relax and consider the potential for grace beyond this challenge. Viewing the experience as a rebirth, she saw an opportunity to be initiated into a new vibration and a heightened level of self-awareness.

Confronting deep-seated emotional issues of unworthiness and abandonment brought to the surface by this incident, Andrea underwent a process akin to peeling back layers of an onion, revealing childhood wounds in need of healing. Shedding old masks and beliefs that no longer served her, she embarked on a journey to discover a profound truth and essence within herself.

Intuitively, I sensed that the Poison Ivy not only impacted Andrea's immune system but symbolized an alchemical release, a transformative burning from within. Forced to surrender, she relinquished control and let go of the belief that her value was tied to her success as a homeowner.

In addition to emotional and spiritual support, I imparted to Andrea the wisdom of the earth, explaining that nature often provides an antidote near poisonous plants. Life always provides a solution within arm's reach of the problem, just like in nature. She found healing in the "plantain" plant growing in her yard, learning a crucial lesson: as we navigate our alchemical journey through life, the earth is a supportive force.

Three years later, Andrea reflected that this initiation had been essential for her growth and marked a clear progression to the next level of her ascension.

Too often, people are not allowed to feel. For most of us, this begins in early childhood. If we were allowed to be with our feelings, experiencing them as they happen without judgment from others, we would feel it, move through it, and then pop out even clearer than before with a new awareness, and simply move on!

Instead, we are often taught it is not an appropriate time, place, or feeling, and then we stuff it down and never allow it to process.

The fact is that unprocessed emotions never go away.

They only go deeper into us and must be dealt with eventually. So, people end up employing all sorts of tactics to numb themselves so they do not deal with the emotion. This only leads to more and more stagnation and blockages and eventually will show up as illness—mental, physical, or spiritual.

This is what creates the first stage of Dissolution. How you go through this phase is up to you.

You can go through it with knowledge and use the many techniques and tools that exist—many of which are described in this book—to transform the density or darkness into light and allow an unfolding of the illumination that is possible. Sometimes, we ignore the signs and the call from our Soul and continue to numb it or stuff it back down. Fear is the major reason why so many choose to avoid these feelings. People will use all sorts of things to avoid feelings: shopping, sex, food, alcohol, drugs, caffeine, intellect, and media—even pharmaceutical drugs have been created to assist in the numbing of feelings instead of actually dealing with the root cause of the pain.

Fear creates a primal response: fight, flight, or freeze. Fear will keep you stuck in the same pattern. We just try and keep doing what we are used to doing, too afraid to change and see what a new way of life could provide for us. So we do everything possible to keep our life functioning the same instead of having the courage to take the time, energy, and resources we have to stop and dive into what is being shown to us.

Open your eyes. Have the courage to see the reality of what is truly being shown to you so you can begin the process of dissolving what no longer serves you.

The unknown can be scary, but it is precisely the place where ANYTHING is possible.

Too often, people try to keep everything the same because they do not want to hurt someone else or are afraid of how someone will react.

The truth is that we are all ONE, and we are all connected. This means that whatever is in YOUR highest good is actually in the highest good for EVERYONE! Miracles can only happen when we choose the path of truth and love over fear.

Sometimes, your words or actions are needed to catalyze someone else into an energy where they can also shift!

Never underestimate the power of your joy. And choosing JOY is the key. That choice to follow your joy might mean that you have to go through a challenging process. As with everything in creation, before something new can be created, the old must die. This is the dissolution.

This process does not happen once in a lifetime but over and over.

In essence, this process is all around us: each minute is a cycle; each day, the Sun dies to the Moon; each week, the Moon changes into a new phase; each season falls to the next. Just as every cell in our body is born and then dies, every thought we have is born and then dies as a new one arises. Your desires will change. Your interests will change. Your ideas will change. Your life will always be changing.

The more you can accept this and embrace it, the sooner you can arrive at a state of peace. For, truly, the only constant in life is change.

This phase will be what some call "darkness," for what we do not "see" within ourselves is where the light is asking to illuminate. All darkness is just the absence of light. And light can be brought to everything. There is nothing that the light—your awareness—cannot illuminate.

So, this stage in your life may see you giving up your career or losing your job. It may be a relationship needs to change or end. A habit that is so engrained needs to stop. It can manifest drastically for some, for they may see themselves losing everything. Or it may only affect one area of your life.

The overall experience feels like your life as you knew it or a part of your identity is falling apart. In this place, emotions such as fear, uncertainty, and the absence of a secure foundation may surface.

Recognize the opportunity for great expansion.

The miracle is on the other side of the unknown. If you can trust enough to surrender in the darkness and do the "work" of dissolving the attachment to what you knew about your life or yourself, you will arrive at a new shore.

Do not get stuck here in the lower frequency, dwelling in the darkness too long, and using substances that actually feed the darkness. With this, you can lose the opportunity and, sadly, end up spiraling deeper into darkness.

A wise person once told me, "You must be willing to give up everything, but you will lose nothing." Wherever you dig your heels in and say, "No, not this!" is where you will stop. Nothing is as important as your Soul's expansion. And that requires complete surrender.

The Seeker seeks the Self…the capital "S" Self…the Higher Self. This is what brings about true, real, and lasting realization.

Along this path, one must uncover all the layers of the small self: all the things one has gathered, put upon, taken in, given away, lied about, sacrificed, conditioned, ignored, and betrayed—as well as the places one has upheld, stood by, been truthful, and honored the sacred.

The "Shadow" are the parts that are hidden, for they are the "negative" of what is seen as light. Realization means looking at it all. The Shadow is the place we start, for you can never realize wholeness without integration of the Shadow.

As you wake up to the fact that you have a responsibility, you also awaken to the delight that you have the power of choice!

The more you illuminate the past burdens you carry, the lighter you become. This allows your whole being on every level to become lighter. And with this, you are able to go "lighter" or ascend.

Attachments pull you down. Worries pull you down. Expectations, ideals, and beliefs can weigh you down if they are not shifting to meet the new awarenesses that are awakening in you.

To continue to elevate, become less attached to what has been. Be content in this moment. Find the serenity in the now. This lightens you! And this creates the ability for your energy body, all levels, to ascend into "higher" frequencies.

There is a nuance here. Does this mean you accept abuse or toxicity or a life circumstance that is less than what you truly desire? No. Do not take your frequency down to the level of that which you are experiencing around you right now, and match your vibration to it! It means you become aware of what "is" in this moment. You listen to your inner knowing, truth, and guidance. Then, you use your discernment, honor yourself, and make a decision about what you are going to do about it. And keep refocusing on the higher perspective.

Tools: Making Space for Transformation

While the first phase of transformation requires aspects of your self (little "s") and life to end…die…dissolve…and shift, centering yourself in sacred daily practices can provide comfort to help your Soul during the time of healing and expansion. It also creates the foundation and container for you to use as you go through the process.

Let's first talk about the Sacred Wheel of the Year, the energetic basis for how we will create the container for your Sacred Space.

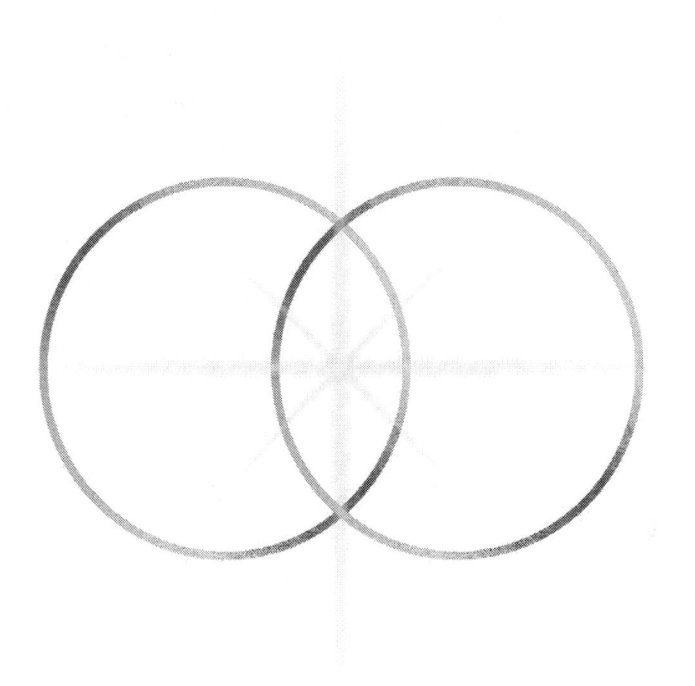

Wheel of the Year

Sabbat	Date	Notes
YULE	Dec 20 - 23	Winter Solstice
IMBOLC	Feb 1 - 2	
OSTARA	March 20 - 23	Spring Equinox
BELTANE	Apr 30 - May 1	
LITHA	June 20 - 23	Summer Solstice
LAMMAS	Aug 1 - 2	
MABON	Sept 20 - 23	Autumn Equinox
SAMHAIN	Oct 31 - Nov 1	

Elements: Air, Fire, Earth, Water

©2019 Sarah Wergin, RN, LAc.

The Sacred Wheel of the Year

The Sacred Wheel of the Year is a neo-pagan system often referred to as the Eight Grove Festivals. It combines the four solar-oriented solstices and equinoxes with the lunar-oriented cross-quarter festivals.

These powerful times reflect the natural cycle of Mother Earth and also the influence of the celestial realm. These energetic qualities influence your body and life, connecting from the Universe above to the season that Mother Earth is moving through below.

The Sacred Wheel of the Year is a powerful tool. Embracing it can change how you move through the cycles of your life, flowing through the seasons.

I also use the Sacred Wheel of the Year to teach the order and method of opening Sacred Space or creating a magic circle. And I believe, as with all things, that everyone needs to find what feels potent and true for them so that their directed focus and intention are clear and powerful.

What I share here is only a helpful starting point. You could adopt it completely, take aspects of it, and use it for your own, or create something completely different. As long as it draws you into your alignment, that is what matters when creating an energetic container or Sacred Space.

Utilizing the eight points of the Sacred Wheel of the Year as a circle involves invoking the directions, encompassing the four cardinal directions along with the cross-quarters, all of which correspond to different seasons.

These seasons can also have different energies that relate to them, like archangels, totems, animals, deities, or themes. These awaken the energies that can help you hold an energetically-protected space. The Wheel moves in a clockwise circle according to the directions.

Sacred Space

Sacred Space can be created anywhere. It is just a place that is quiet, where you can be alone with your own energy, and creates a "sealed" container for your spiritual work. This can be a room in your house, a tent on your lawn, or a spot in the woods. And anything in between.

You energetically cleanse this space to support the conditions that allow for clear connection with the Divine and your Higher Self, free of any outside influences that are less than Divine love, light, and truth. Grounded in that space of purity, you can safely open up to give thanks, receive guidance, or do healing/clearing work.

As you journey on your path of exploration, these ideas become your tools…which become action…which creates magic. When you master this, you will see how everything you think, say, and do becomes your means of creation for your life.

But the first steps on the path are to learn and practice. For the purpose of opening Sacred Space, we call in the four cardinal directions that relate to the four elements: Earth, Air, Water, and Fire. Which element you place in which direction depends on the tradition you use. A Native American tradition puts elements in different directions than the Avalonian tradition. And they put the elements in different directions than the Western Hermetic tradition. Which element you call upon in which direction is about feeling into what each direction feels like to you.

You could also just open Sacred Space by using only the directions or elements by themselves. I have found that magic, when it is layered, creates more power. So, I layer it with many different elements or aspects, as you'll see in the sample invocation at the end of this section. That is why I choose the season relating to each direction, then the element related to that direction, then the animal, totems, qualities, archangels, and the gods or goddesses. Each one of the directions and all our "helpers" are being invited to hold sacred space for our container to do our alchemical work.

Remember that belief equals potency equals power!

> *As above, So below.*
> —Thoth, Ancient of Days

Connecting to the Goddess

In Western culture, the last 2,000-plus years have had a heavy emphasis on the patriarchal system of what Divinity is. The current awakening of the Sacred Feminine that is happening on the planet is the resurrection of the Goddess back into our awareness, vocabulary, culture, and spirituality.

The Goddess aspect of Creator/Source is coming out of the shadows and is rising in union with the God aspect of Creator/Source. With this, we need to remember the devotional practices of the Goddess traditions and integrate them to once again restore balance in our daily lives and within ourselves.

Awakening your consciousness is an alchemical process that is all about the union of your inner God/masculine and Goddess/feminine aspects. Practicing these ancient High Holy Festivals can support that process. Acknowledging that these festival times are influenced by our Earth seasons and the energies of the Sun and Moon restores a powerful connection between the human body, mind, and spirit.

The Festivals

Our Sacred Wheel that we "turn" acknowledges (1) the solstices and the equinoxes (solar) and (2) the cross-quarters (lunar). Studying these will help you experience the subtle changes that move us and guide our inner energies, showing us why we express what we do in the world at different times of the year.

In ancient times, the year was thought to be divided into two halves: the "dark" half, or winter starting at Samhain, and the "light" half, or summer starting at Beltane. The Festivals were very much tied to celebrating power points of the year as they related to agricultural and nomadic lifestyles. It was important to worship at certain times to give thanks for fertility and harvests because their survival depended on it. They also helped clans plan when they would be able to get together and trade goods when the weather was likely to permit traveling, when they could move and manage livestock and plan for their agricultural practices.

While the Solar festival dates are Germanic in origin, they became adapted over time by the Celtic Britons when the Anglo-Saxon invasions began around the 5th century CE. Originally, the Lunar Festivals were only observed by the ancient Celts, thus reflecting the more Goddess-centered belief system.

Instead of ignoring the natural rhythms that dictated our ancestors' lives or only honoring a Lunar or Solar Holy Day, we must reclaim our connection to the Earth and the stars—and use the energies latent in all these High Holy Days to evolve and heal our lives.

For me, these eight power days (also known by Neopagans as the Eight Grove Festivals) collectively carry the balance of the Divine Union that creates our experience of living here on Earth. Honoring both the Solar and Lunar circuits.

Autumn Equinox
Mabon (September 22/23)
Samhain (October 31/November 1)

These are harvest festivals. Mabon is when the hours of day and night are equal, moving toward the evenings growing longer. Samhain marks the end of the year and the beginning of the new year cycle. Both begin the "dark" half of the year, going inward and being quiet.

MABON

Corresponding Life Stage: Matriarch
Harvesting the intention/effort.

KNOWING THYSELF. The culmination of another year on your Soul path. Take time to recognize yourself. Balance output and input as you wind down this cycle. It is time to give thanks for all you have experienced and all that has come to you.

Energies & Symbols:

Mabon is the festival of the harvest and honoring Mother Earth. The Autumn Equinox, celebrated on September 22/23, is the time of year when daylight and nighttime are equal. We honor Ertha, Gaia, Lady of the Lake/Creator of the Mists.

Stand barefoot to feel Mother Gaia below and to ground yourself in Her stability and healing. Do a meditation to breathe the Earth's energies into your body and fill yourself with Her nurturing.

This season is ruled by the Mother energy. It is a good time of year to connect with any matrons in your life, such as grandmothers, mothers, aunties, etc.

As the year starts to wane, think about what you are letting go of from this year and what you are calling forth to "become" as your dedication to the next year and cycle.

Mabon is the counterpoint of the year to the Spring Equinox, Ostara/Ostre. It is the time of year we celebrate harvesting before the first frost occurs. It signals the end of summer and beginning of autumn. The days are still warm, but the nights are chilly. The life in the plants begins to die back and the animals start to fatten themselves.

The Equinoxes are a time of intensified psychic stress. And I will also say, from an Oriental Medicine perspective, a time of overall body/mind stress.

As you shift gears between seasons, your body/mind must adjust to the new energies. Receiving supportive therapies, such as acupuncture, can help the mind and body shift into the new frequency of the season with more ease and grace.

This season carries the energy of the spiral, representing rebirth and the Divine cycle of life and death in all things.

Symbols of Mabon:

+ Festival: Mabon/Autumn Equinox, September 22/23
+ Direction: West
+ Element: Earth (Avalonian)/Water (Western Hermetic, Native American-Lakota)
+ Color: Brown/Orange (Avalonian)/Black (Native American-Lakota)
+ Goddess/Archangel: Juno/Hera, Gabriel
+ Symbol: Orb, Crystal Ball
+ Animal: Bear, Fox, Badger
+ Herbs: Rose, Milkweed, Myrrh, Sage, Solomon's Seal
+ Flowers: Rose, Marigolds, Thistle, Ferns
+ Tree: White Poplar, Vine
+ Food: Grains of all kinds, Corn, Nuts, Beans, Apples, Potatoes, Carrots
+ Phrase: "Gentle Endings, Introspection, Our Shadow Side"

SAMHAIN

Corresponding Life Stage: Crone
The Shadow time.

Known as the Celtic New Year and celebrated October 31/November 1. To the ancient Celts, it was an in-between day, beyond the veil. This time of year guides us inward to begin the process of inner reflection. The season, as it is coming to the end of the harvest and the foliage is dying back, tells us to go down to our roots, too. Rest, be quiet, and restore yourself. Take stock of what you have inside.

This slow time of the year also offers us the presence to dive into our "Shadow" aspects and see what is lying in the darkness there—judgments, wounds, things we're embarrassed or ashamed of—and needs to be welcomed into the light.

What is causing any pain in your life? What are you still hiding from?

Energies & Symbols:

It is a time of honoring (not ignoring!) the dark side of life, the Shadow sides of ourselves, death, and our ancestors. Until you have explored this aspect of yourself, you cannot hold in a state of light! It will tug at you until you invite it in.

In this season, the Goddess rules decay, darkness, and death. She is the guardian of the gateways to the otherworld. The world beyond this earthly life.

This time of year, the sun is lower in the southern sky and the days become shorter. The air is cooling, and the foliage of trees and other plants is turning to beautiful rays of yellow, orange, red, and brown, then falling to the ground and darkening to black. They decompose and return nutrients to the earth in this ageless cycle of death and rebirth. Birds start to gather and begin their journey to warmer climates, and animals start to eat more and prepare for the long, cold nights of winter.

Samhain is the time when we stand before the Dark Mother of the Underworld and surrender to Her powers of transformation and regeneration. It is the time to let go of all that no longer serves us and to prepare for a new beginning. We honor the many faces of Death and recognize the fact that everything material will change and die in its original form to make way for the new to be reborn. The Crone carries the wisdom of our loving Grandmother, who teaches us all the ways of the Goddess and Her nature and also shows us how to accept with grace all the challenges his life will offer.

She invites us to meet her deep in the earth cave and to sit before the cauldron with Her. To discover all the things that we have hidden away, covered up so no one can see—even ourselves. All the parts of ourselves we have disowned or forgotten.

She may leave us there for a time, feeling abandoned or alone. But this part of the journey we must do alone. Then, when we are ready, She will return in all of Her light and glory, and we will see the true beauty that was there all along in the darkness. We will know why we traveled there, to the underworld.

Samhain is the time of year when primitive pastoralists had to decide which herd would be slaughtered because keeping them all through the winter was impossible. Crops also had to be gathered by October 31—anything not harvested by then was abandoned.

This is when the veil between the worlds is very thin! The doors of the *sidhe-* (shee) mounds were open, and neither fairy nor human need any magical words to come and go. This is also a time when spirits of the dead can come and sit by the Samhain fire and commune with living loved ones.

Symbols of Samhain:

+ Festival: Samhain, October 31/November 1
+ Direction: Northwest
+ Element: -
+ Color: Black (Avalonian)
+ Goddess/Archangel: Sheela Na Gig, Keridewen (Cerridwen), Kali, Nephthys, Morta
+ Symbol: Sickle, Cauldron, Scissors
+ Animal: Bat, Black Cat, Crow
+ Herbs: Wormwood, Hazel, Thistle
+ Flowers: Marigolds, Chrysanthemums
+ Tree: Reed
+ Food: Apples, Pomegranates, Pumpkins, Squash, Corn, Cider, Mulled Wine
+ Phrase: "The Grandmother Crone"

Winter Solstice
Yule (December 20/21)
Imbolc (February 1/2)

These are mid-winter festivals. Yule is the longest night of the year. While Imbolc can feel like the deepest part of the winter, there are usually signs of new growth just under the surface, marking the midpoint between the beginning of winter and the beginning of summer as celebrated by Celtic cultures.

YULE

Corresponding Life Stage: Infant
Flame in the Darkness.

It is a time of the "Life within Death" aspect of the Goddess, as this is the longest night of the year, and then the days start to increase again. This time is about holding the Light of hope and renewal, lighting your way toward rebirth. After this power point day, the daylight begins to increase. Still in the depths of winter, you see glimpses of warmth.

Energies & Symbols:

As we enter the season of ice and snow, we see our landscape change into a wonderland of white and silver. The richness of the green pine stands out and reminds us that there is life to celebrate. It is a time to be still and use the energy of the land to quiet our minds and go within to contemplate our spiritual life.

A time for rest, to eat heavier foods so they may keep our bodies warm, and to sit by a fire and just let the activity of our mind, body, and life slow. A time for accepted leisure. Our bodies and minds need this season to process all the activity of the warmer months and help us build up our reserves for the coming seasons.

Increasing rest, food, and sleep are ways to honor our bodies and Souls. Time spent in the close company of friends and family and to welcome any in-need strangers, as well. Where the Crone leads us to our symbolic death (the death of the old self), this is the stillness before return to form.

The Sacred Feminine/Goddess aspect here is the silver shining face of stillness. The time to "stand still" and dwell in quiet, rest, and inner contemplation. It is the season to look back and evaluate the past year, your accomplishments, and experiences. The warm, calm, encompassing face of comfort that wraps us in Her blanket of white chills the air and tells us to go inside and rest in our inner sanctum. The Earth is at rest, mirroring to us the request to do so, too.

Use this time to slow down and spend more time in meditation, contemplation, and prayer, walking in nature, sitting in front of the fire—or even just lighting a candle and doing nothing!

It is more important than ever to not rely on our technology to light up every room into the late night hours or make yourself "busy" on your handheld device. It is Her giving you the permission to put away the distractions, sit in the darkness, rest in contemplation, make some meals from scratch, take that stolen nap, read a comforting book, or sit outside and gaze at the night sky.

Use this time given to you wisely, for once spring arrives, your focus will be "action" again.

Symbols of Yule:

- Festival: Yule/Winter Solstice December 20/21
- Direction: North
- Element: Air (Avalonian, Native American-Lakota)/Earth (Western Hermetic)
- Color: Silver (Avalonian)/White (Native American-Lakota)
- Goddess/Archangel: Ceres/Demeter, Uriel
- Symbol: Sword, Feather Fan
- Animal: Owl, Great White Buffalo
- Herbs: Ginger, Cinnamon, Nutmeg, Cloves, Rosemary, Peppermint
- Flowers: Mistletoe, Holly, Ivy, Poinsettia
- Tree: Yew, Mistletoe, Birch

- Food: Apples, Pears, Nuts, Dries Fruit, Mulled Wines
- Phrase: "Purity, Cleansing, and Our Sacred Path"

IMBOLC/IMBOLG

Corresponding Life Stage: Child
Breakthroughs.

Celebrated around February 1/2, your innocence is restored as you emerge from the deep "Shadow" work, and you can look at life in a whole new way. You have a fresh perspective on your life and self. You have the energy to start thinking about what you want to change and create in your life.

You are ready for a new beginning.

Energies & Symbols:

For some cultures, this marks the end of winter. At this festival, we celebrate the LIGHT. In the phases of the Goddess, this is the aspect of the Maid: the child full of hope, anticipation, passion, creativity, and fertile potential.

The Goddess most known to preside over this festival is Brigid, aka Bride, Brighde, Brigit, Bridget, or St. Brigid to the Christians, who lived about 453-523 AD.

Brigid was a goddess of the Tuatha Dé Danann, the Shining Ones, who were a race that carried much ancient wisdom and gifts. She was a daughter of the chief of the gods, The Dagda, and was known as a Goddess of healers, poets, smiths, childbirth, and inspiration. Her name means "exalted one."

She is a Triple Goddess, meaning she carries within her all the phases of the Goddess, Maid-Mother-Crone. The triple spiral is one of her symbols:

Imbolc has been traditionally associated with the onset of lactation of ewes, soon to give birth to the spring lambs. This could vary by as much as two weeks before or after the start of February. The timing of agrarian festivals can vary widely, given regional variations in climate. This has led to some debate about the festival's timing and origins.

The holiday was, and for many still is, a festival of the hearth and home and a celebration of the lengthening days and the early signs of spring. Celebrations often involved hearth fires, special foods, divination or watching for omens, and candles or a bonfire if the weather permitted. Fire and purification were important parts of the festival. The lighting of candles and fires represented the return of warmth and the increasing power of the Sun over the coming months.

The first lambs of the year are born, and the milk of the ewe signals the return of life in winter. People would look forward to having milk again to supplement the preserved winter diet. It is a time to pour milk as an offering on Her sacred lands, bake and share barley cakes, write poetry, and return to merriment!

This phase of the Goddess teaches us that no one is a victim. We create our lives and have choice each moment of each day. She teaches us that we need to take responsibility for our lives being what they are now. And that by taking back this responsibility, we also take back our power to do something about it! A child lives in the moment, feels their emotion, goes through the temper tantrum, and, when it is complete, just as quickly finds the things they love and returns to wonder and play in the world.

She is also the healer, bringing us back to our true Self through this process. The one that got lost through the years of conditioning that adulthood can create and allows for the return of our wholeness by welcoming the integration of our inner child. All those years of living are to bring about the best "vintage" of you.

We long for springtime and wait for Bridget to touch us with the white rod and bring us renewal. We can now express more love and compassion for ourselves and others and put it into action in the world.

Symbols of Imbolc:

- Festival: Imbolc February 1/2
- Direction: Northeast
- Element: -
- Color: White (Avalonian)
- Goddess/Archangel: Bridget
- Symbol: Spindle, Spinning Wheel
- Animal: Swan, Phoenix, Unicorn, Cow, Ewe
- Herbs: Ginger, Cinnamon, Chili Peppers, Garlic, Onion
- Flowers: Rowan, Snowdrop
- Tree: Rowan
- Food: Dairy, Barley Cakes, Spicy Food, Spiced Wine
- Phrase: "The Maiden"

Spring Equinox
Ostara (March 20/21/22)
Beltane (April 30/May 1)

These are fertility festivals. Ostara is when the hours of day and night are again equal, with days growing longer. Beltane is directly opposite Samhain, marking the beginning of the "light" half of the year. It is another "between" day when the veil is said to be thin, as with Samhain.

OSTARA/EOSTRE

Corresponding Life Stage: Maiden
Renewed Vision.

Your new self is moving into the world. You are rejuvenated, restored, and ready to plant seeds of what you want to create in your life.

Energies & Symbols:

Ostara/Oestre/Ostare is the Vernal Equinox. When the light of day and dark of night are equal. Celebrated around March 20/21/22, it is the festival that honors the Goddesses Artha, Grainne, Sulis, and Minerva.

Where Imbolc represents the first stirrings of the Goddess awakening from the deep inner time of winter and the underworld or the newly birthed child, Ostara can be seen as Her being fully awake and blossoming into a young woman.

Traditionally, fertility rites fall at Beltane, as does vegetation fertility, as the first sprouts from the seeds that were sowed at Imbolc begin to show. But Ostara can be a flirtatious time; our own sensual stirrings start to awaken, and we feel a sense of excitement and anticipation about life.

The name Easter came from the Teutonic goddess Eostre, whose name was also a variation of Ishtar, Astarte, and Aset (Isis).

Ostara is the time of year we make our wands of power. It is a symbol of our inner fire, a festival ruled by the element of fire. It is a symbol of virility and fertility—an extension of the Goddess and arm of the owner to direct focused intention where desired.

Symbols of Ostara:

+ Festival: Ostara March 20/21/22
+ Direction: East
+ Element: Fire (Avalonian, Native American-Lakota)/Air (Western Hermetic)
+ Color: Green/Gold (Avalonian)/Yellow (Native American-Lakota)
+ Goddess/Archangel: Vesta/Hestia, Raphael
+ Symbol: Wand
+ Animal: Rabbit, Hare, Golden Eagle, Woodpecker
+ Herbs: Olive Leaf
+ Flowers: Daffodil, Violet, Iris, Tulip, Hyacinth, Crocus
+ Tree: Gorse, Alder

- Food: Seeds, Nuts, Sprouts, Leafy Greens, Eggs
- Phrase: "New Beginnings, Clarity, and Illumination"

BELTANE/BELTAINE/BELLTAINE/BELTINE

Corresponding Life Stage: Lover
Flowing Passion.

Beltane is the most powerful time for joy, pleasure, and love. It is the season when passions run high, and you feel vibrant and alive—dancing in beauty, pleasure, joy, and love. You feel excited for your life ahead.

Your creative juices are flowing, and your power is expanding.

Energies & Symbols:

This is the time of year when everything and everyone starts to awaken from the sleep of winter. Our passions, juices, creativity, lust, and cravings are in full potency. We are celebrating the Queen of May or Hawthorn woman. Known as Rhiannon, Goddess of love and sexuality, who is Fairy Queen and rides a white horse and tempts the Welsh Lord Pwyll, or Blodeuwedd, who is both flower maiden and owl goddess.

Like the sap in the trees and the blossoming of the flowers, our fertile, creative energies are strong and clear.

The original meaning is "Bel-fire" after the Celtic God "Bel," the God of light and fire, and the fires were first lit by the High King on Tara Hill in Pagan Ireland. Bel is the British-Celtic equivalent of the Gaulish-Celtic Cernunnos, represented as a Horned God, god of animals, aka the Stag.

Traditionally, we are celebrating the mating of the Goddess and God in Sacred Union and ritual marriage called the Great Marriage. It is a celebration of the return of life and fertility. But remember, this Great Marriage, as all Pagan marriages, is for one year and a day. That commitment is reevaluated at that time. All things were done with the consent of the Mother Goddess and to serve Her and Her nature, and in the next cycle, it may serve to mate with another.

Beltane fires were lit on hills and danced around and jumped over to bring husbands or wives by pregnant mothers for easy delivery, and cows would walk on the ashes for good milk yield.

Dancing around the Maypole with colored ribbons of white, red, yellow, and black representing the four phases of the Goddess: The Maid-The Lover-The Mother-The Crone. Or as a way to honor the sacred marriage of the God and Goddess and celebrate fertility.

Precious to alchemists is the fresh morning dew (or rain) during the month of April-May. The energy stored in this potent elixir that has soaked up all the power of the moon and then charged with the energy of the season of regeneration and gathered on the sacred plants is a miracle. Walk outside in the morning barefoot and get your hands wet with the morning dew that has collected on a plant, then press into the face or anywhere on your body to anoint yourself with this potent elixir.

Symbols of Beltane:

+ Festival: Beltane April 30/May 1
+ Direction: Southeast
+ Element: -
+ Color: Red (Avalonian)
+ Goddess/Archangel: Rhiannon, Venus, Aphrodite, Pele
+ Symbol: Comb, Mirror
+ Animal: White Horse, Swallows, Doves, Frogs, Owl
+ Herbs: St. John's Wort
+ Flowers: Hawthorn, Honeysuckle, Woodruff
+ Tree: Willow
+ Food: Dairy, Oatmeal Cakes
+ Phrase: "The Lover"

Summer Solstice
Litha (June 20/21/22)
Lughnasadh/Lammas (August 1/2)

These are midsummer festivals. Litha is the longest day of the year. Lughnasadh (or Lammas) is the peak of summer and its bounty, marking the midpoint between the beginning of summer and the beginning of winter, as celebrated by Celtic cultures.

LITHA

Corresponding Life Stage: Partner
Abundant Light.

You are embodying your truth as you live your life in your full essence and expression. You are overflowing with energy and substance. You feel glorious, vibrant, and strong. Even if you are dealing with a lot, you have a sense of resources supporting you.

Energies & Symbols:

This time of year, we celebrate the festival of Litha-Summer Solstice around June 20/21/22, the water aspect of the Goddess and also the Light of the Sun God. This is the longest day of the year, and so it is the full expression of Yang/masculine/light energy of the Sun God, or the full creative force of the Goddess overflowing with her watery elixir.

At Midsummer, the Oak King, God of the Waxing year, falls to the Holly King, God of the Waning year. It is the peak blaze of light and warmth. In ancient times, the human enactor of the Oak King was sacrificed in actuality, and it was a great honor to be chosen as this sacrifice. All year long, the chosen male was treated like a God and King and given the best of everything. And at this time of year, he was then sacrificed.

Unlike the God, the Goddess never dies. She only presents us with different faces and aspects of Herself throughout the year. This festival reveals to us Her watery aspect, the fullest potential of life. This is truly a festival of fire and water.

This being a water and fire holy day, it is important to have a fire (or at least a burning candle) as well as a chalice, cauldron, or goblet of water to honor the Goddess. The chalice symbolizes the feminine aspect of receiving energy and also the watery aspect of Creator. It is a time of year to keep with the ancient tradition and practice the ceremonies or rituals "skyclad" or naked.

The Goddesses honored at this time include Domnu, Vivienne, Aphrodite, Nimue, Sedna, Sulis, and Minerva.

Symbols of Midsummer:

+ Festival: Litha June 20/21/22
+ Direction: South
+ Element: Water (Avalonian)/Fire (Native American/Western Hermetic)
+ Color: Blue (Avalonian)/Red (Native American-Lakota)
+ Goddess/Archangel: Pallas/Athena, Michael
+ Symbol: Bodies of Water, Sea Animals, Chalice
+ Animal: Blue Heron, Coyote, Snake, Fireflies
+ Herbs: Mugwort, Thyme, Chamomile, Ivy, Fern
+ Flowers: Vervain, Chamomile, Rose, Lily, Lavender, Yarrow, Daisy, Carnation, Primrose
+ Tree: Oak, Heather
+ Food: Fresh Fruit
+ Phrase: "Passion, Creativity, and New Ideas"

LUGHNASADH/LAMMAS

Corresponding Life Stage: Mother
Receiving abundance.

Focus on opening yourself up to receive. All your effort and time is coming to fruition. Set the stage for opening and surrender. Allow all good things to come to you. As you bask in the sun of your harvest, seeing your seeds fruiting, make sure you look around and enjoy this time.

Energies & Symbols:

This is the season when we celebrate the first harvest and abundance from the Goddess. It was traditionally held on the day of the first harvest of the year, usually August 1/2, to celebrate the abundance, fruition, and life-giving nature of the Goddess and give thanks for the nurturing and nourishment from her womb.

We honor the Mother aspect, the Provider, the Nurturer, and the Sustainer as Ceres/Demeter, Ker the Grain Mother, and Madron/Modron/Madryn.

This time of year, take a moment to pay homage to the Mother Mary and Magdalene of history…the desecrated, hidden, and abandoned Mother/Goddess figure in the Christian tradition.

Or maybe you feel called to honor InAnna or Isis as Mother, Queen of Heaven, the Creator Goddess who actually seeded us!

It's that season when we acknowledge and celebrate the essence of motherhood and the birth of various facets of life. This extends beyond the traditional notion of giving birth to children and includes the creation of anything meaningful in one's life. Many women express their nurturing abilities not only through motherhood but also by giving life to careers, projects, or by providing care to individuals, plants, or animals in diverse ways. It's a time to rejoice in the creation of all forms.

Lugh is also the name of a fire/light God and may be derived from *Lux,* Latin for "light." He is the same God as Baal (Egyptian), Belos (Greek), Bel (Babylonian), and Balor (Celtic). We honor His part in this Festival, as the Sun rays that are so strong at this time are creating the heat and golden colors all around us. The last burning heat of his light and strength before He dies, like the grain/corn that gives us nourishment to sustain us through the dark months.

Symbols of Lughnasadh:

+ Festival: Lughnasadh/Lammas August 1/2
+ Direction: Southwest
+ Element: -
+ Color: Yellow (Avalonian)
+ Goddess/Archangel: Ker, Mary, Ertha, Gaia, Madron/Modron/Madryn
+ Symbol: Chalice, Loom, Shuttle
+ Animal: Song Thrush, Deer, Stag
+ Herbs: Heather, Aloe, Rose, Sandalwood
+ Flowers: Heather, Rose
+ Tree: Hazel
+ Food: Grains of all kinds, Berries, Acorns, Crabapples, Apples, Grapes, Pears
+ Phrase: "The Mother"

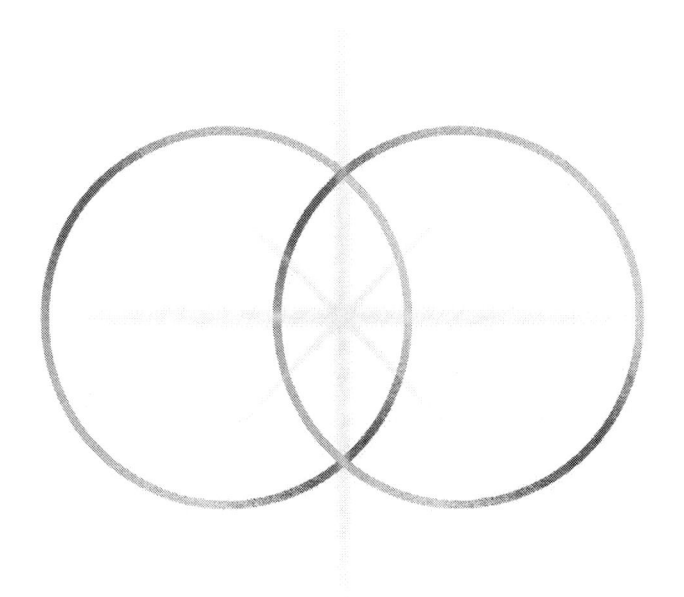

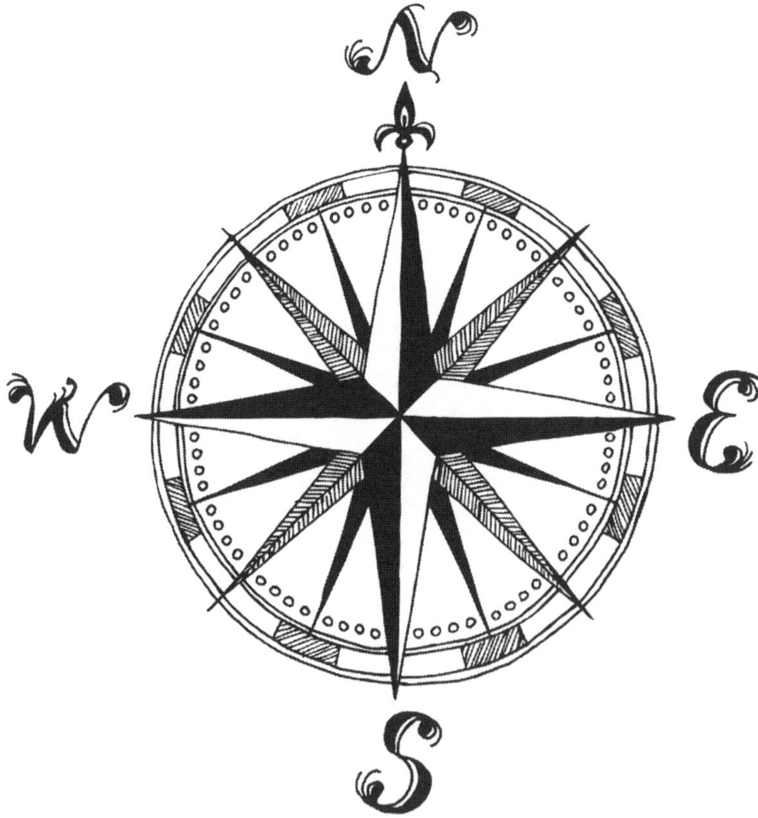
N
W
E
S

The Meaning of the Directions

The power points in the Sacred Wheel of the Year all correlate to aspects that rule them, including color, navigational direction, and natural elements.

Each tradition is a little different. One tradition will acknowledge that SOUTH is FIRE, and another will say it is WATER. Neither is right nor wrong. Below are a few examples of different traditions and their respective associations.

Remember: the following are simply guidelines.

You put into each direction what FEELS right for you! *For power will follow your feeling.*

You must take the time to learn and feel to find out what is right for YOU. These are just starting points for exploration.

Start by getting familiar with these concepts, studying them, and practicing. Over time, you will discover and develop your own associations with the Sacred Wheel.

This is another one of your tools to support you in living your truth and manifesting the reality that you desire and, ultimately, embodying the Divinity that you are.

For now, just look at these "maps" and start to understand why things are placed in a particular area.

Avalonian Tradition

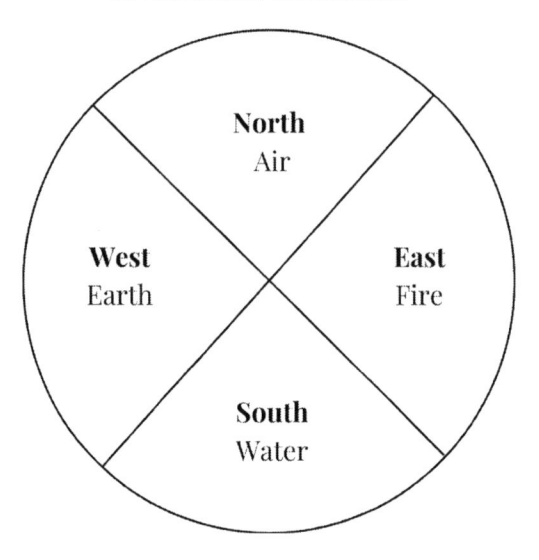

- **North** — Air
- **West** — Earth
- **East** — Fire
- **South** — Water

Hermetic Tradition

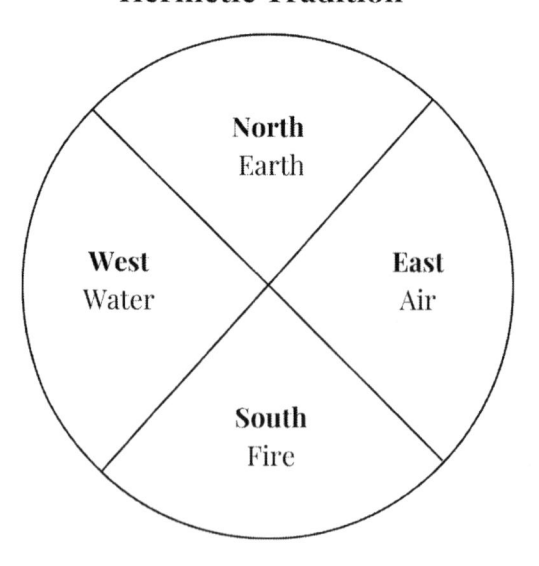

- **North** — Earth
- **West** — Water
- **East** — Air
- **South** — Fire

Lakota/Sioux Native American Tradition

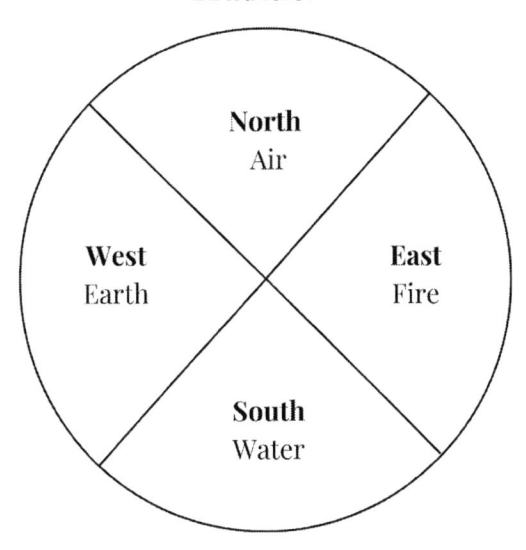

```
         North
          Air

West              East
Earth             Fire

         South
         Water
```

Fire is about our passions, excitement, and zest for life. Creativity.

Earth is about our nourishment, where we are supported or taken care of. Our foundation and stability.

Air brings in change, thoughts, and ideas.

Water is about cleansing and washing you clean of the past and what no longer serves.

East: Illumination

The Sun rises in the East, the direction of the first light. The awakening of our Soul and the new beginning of our life on this path toward the sacred.

South: Passion

The heat and passion that drives creativity and abundance of all kinds. Awakened Goddess and God energies. Divine Union fully reemerged in our lives.

West: Knowledge

Understanding when it is time to go inward to discover truth, to honor the stillness and the grace to let all things come to an end with gratitude.

North: Dedication

The pure path of living a life of devotion and commitment to our Sacred Path.

Mother Earth/Gaia: Unconditional Love and Healing

Honor Her for Her beauty, bounty, and the wisdom She has to take our energies that are less than love and transmute them.

Sky/Star Nations: Guidance and Protection

The knowledge, belief, and trust that we are always looked after.

Sample Invocation

Calling in the directions with their qualities gives them power. Call the energies or qualities that apply in each direction (See Symbols of the Seasons in the previous section for help) and words of power that resonate within you. Otherwise, this "invoking" is just words and not intentional creation.

Opening Sacred Space

Light your candle.

Light your incense (for example, white sage, palo santo, frankincense, myrrh, etc.)

Face each direction as you turn in a clockwise ("Deosil" or "Sunwise") circle. Always start by FACING EAST. This is the direction of renewed light.

(Facing East)

"I call to the direction of the East, of new beginnings and illumination. To Golden Eagle, Mighty Archangel Raphael, and the Goddess Vesta/Hestia Temple Priestess. To the element of AIR. Please hold sacred space. Thank you, Thank you, Thank you."

(Facing Southeast)

"To Rhiannon, the Beltane goddess, the lover. Please hold sacred space, thank you, thank you, thank you."

(Facing South)

"To the direction of the South, of passion, creativity, and new ideas. To snake and coyote, to the Mighty Archangel Michael and the Goddess Pallas/Athena of wisdom and courage. To the element of FIRE. Please hold sacred space. Thank you, thank you, thank you."

(Facing Southwest)

"To the Lammas/Lughnasadh, Goddess Ertha, the mother. Please hold sacred space. Thank you, thank you, thank you."

(Facing West)

"To the direction of the West, our Shadow side, gentle endings and going inward. To bear, Andromeda, to the mighty Archangel Gabriel and the Goddess Juno/Hera, Queen in your own right. To the element of WATER. Please hold sacred space. Thank you, thank you, thank you."

(Facing Northwest)

"To the crone, grandmother goddess of Samhain, Sheila ne Gig. Please hold sacred space. Thank you, thank you, thank you."

(Facing North)

"To the direction of the North, to our sacred path, purity, and cleansing. To the Great White Buffalo, to Owl. To the Mighty Archangel Uriel and the Goddess Ceres/Demeter, provider of abundance. To the element of EARTH. Please hold sacred space. Thank you, thank you, thank you."

(Facing Northeast)

"To the Imbolc goddess, the maiden Bridget. Please hold sacred space. Thank you, thank you, thank you."

(Touch the ground)

"To the Mother Earth below, Gaia, Mother Nature, Lady of Avalon, Isis, Neith, Inanna/Ishtar, Hathor, Shakti, Kwan Yin, Sarasvati, the Magdalene, Mother Mary, Astarte, Hecate, Circe, Durga, Kali. Thank you for your wisdom, unconditional love, and passion. Thank you for your nurturing, sustenance, and the beauty and healing of your nature. Flow through me and rise!"

(Raise arms to the sky)

"To the Father above, the Star Nations, our ancestors and lineage. To Shiva, Yeshua/Sananda, Sanat Kumara, Thoth, Gwyn ap Nudd, and Osiris. Thank you for your protection and guidance. In Divine Union Within. Please hold sacred space. Thank you, thank you, thank you. Blessed Be. AIM."

Now you are ready to sit and practice your ceremony, ritual, meditation, and/or prayer time.

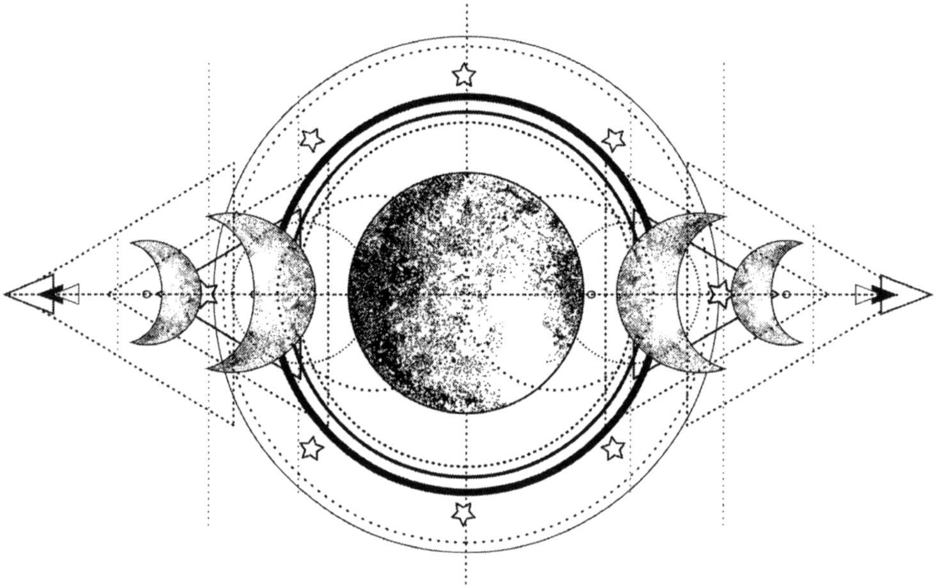

Ceremony

Ceremony is your time to commune with the Divine intentionally for a period of time. It can be as simple or extravagant as you want. It can be 15 minutes of meditation, pulling an oracle card, saying a short prayer, or even conducting an hour-long ritual to manifest abundance. It can look different even from one day to the next.

Ceremony is meant to be one of your most precious and powerful foundational tools to help you stay aligned, centered, and embodied in your Divine Union.

It always amazes me how, if I miss a time, I can feel myself getting thrown off center. Things in the external world can bother me more and cause more worry, anxiety, or distortion. Creating a daily, if not twice a day, practice can create stability for your mind, body, and Soul.

This is why it is common for many religious or spiritual traditions to have twice-a-day designated times devoted to coming to an altar, going into that still place, or deep devotional practice. This brings the awareness inward to the truth of who you are and to Source, which is larger than just you, restoring a sense of connection.

The important first step for a ceremony or ritual is opening Sacred Space.

This is when you call in your "helpers" and Sacred Guardians to create a space in which only Love, Light, and Truth are present for you to do your spiritual "work." While all vibrations are part of the Divine, we want to be working in the light for the greatest good of all.

That is why this step is so important.

Even though we may be "clearing" things that may be lower in vibration, we are releasing them into the light for transformation. The Divine has the power to transmute anything into Love and Light.

Sample Invocation

Consider these as helpful guidelines just to get started. Create what FEELS right for you!

Come into your space and light your candle.

From that candle, light your incense.

Do your "Opening Sacred Space" ritual (see page 75).

Clear yourself and let go of anything you may be holding on to that is less than Love and Light, any heaviness. Check your body! It tells you. Any place feel tight or heavy? Go there and breathe it out…shout it out, cough it out, chant it out, tone it out, cry it out…just make noise to move the energy out! You can jump, dance, move, shake in some way. Or take a Black Obsidian and rub on that area while you breathe. Do whatever feels right. Learn how to clear and heal yourself. Using sound can be very helpful. Toning, chanting, singing, screaming, crying, and even yelling can help move stagnant energy.

When you feel clear…and only then! It may take 5 minutes or 50 minutes…and when you are centered, focus on the stillness, go into meditation, or begin your prayers. Any sacred work you want to undertake can begin at this time.

Sometimes it is enough just to get recentered. If you are feeling some emotion, just acknowledge and integrate them! Emotions are not meant to stay buried. Allow them to surface. DO NOT TRY TO FIGURE OUT WHAT OR WHY you are feeling something. Just let it out. It could be an old emotion from long ago. It could be something that you took on that was not yours. It could be an emotion you are clearing for the planet. It could be an imprint you are clearing from your ancestors. DO NOT try to figure it out because it slows the process and can actually engrain it deeper because your mind will attach to it.

Other times, you may need guidance or want clarity for something. You have the ability to connect to your Higher Self and the Divine to access that information. Or you may be actively drawing something into your life.

This is what ceremony, ritual, or prayer time (whatever you want to call it) is for. Clearing our STUFF, recentering, creating, and giving thanks as if it has already come to be—and giving thanks again!

This is also a good time to do a Tarot reading or pull an oracle card for the day. Ask, "What do I need to do or know today?" and pull a card, read it, and set it on your altar. Contemplate it during your day. You will be surprised.

Then, when you feel complete, close the Sacred Space. This can be done in many ways. Start with the last direction you opened with and then turn counterclockwise/widdershins as you thank them and say three times, "I release you, I release you, I release you."

The quickest is to simply say: "Thank you to all the Divine Beings, Guardians, Guides, Elements, and Directions I have called in. Thank you for holding Sacred Space. I release you. I release you. I release you."

Also, if you leave your space and forget to close it, just bring your awareness back to your space, thank everyone, and imagine closing it. And it is done.

Extinguish your candle with a snuffer (DO NOT blow out—it is said that using two elements against each other can have a negative influence on the magic you just created), and you are complete.

Meditation

At the most basic level, meditation is simply focused attention. That concentrated, clear focus—whether on your breath, your steps while walking, your gaze on a flame, or reciting a mantra—keeps you in the present moment and brings you back to that present moment over and over again. The benefits of daily meditation on physical, mental, and emotional health are widely known, documented, and studied.

Spiritually, meditation is essential to healing, growth, and transformation. It helps us to release stuck emotions and thought patterns, calm the nervous system, and elevate our vibration. This opens us up to receive.

There are countless ways to meditate. Having worked with thousands of clients over the years at various stages in the alchemical process, I recommend that you find one that feels right for you. The most important thing is that you DO IT. If you do not like it, you won't do it. Therefore, find a practice you can go to for calming your mind and getting you recentered in times of stress.

Here are some you can try:

Transcendental Meditation: Silent recitations of a mantra.

Ishayas Ascension: This is the one that resonated most with my Soul and changed my life. This tradition uses silent affirmations or attitudes that you choose to redirect your mind onto that relate to Praise, Gratitude, Love, and Compassion.

Circular breathing can be a form of meditation (sometimes called "Box Breathing" or the "Four-Fold Breath"). This is also used to center oneself before ceremony or ritual. Here are the steps:

1. Close your eyes, bring your awareness inside, and focus on breathing.
2. As you inhale, feel your abdomen expand and try to get your breath down into your lower abdomen. Try to make your inhale last for the count of four seconds.

3. Then, when you have inhaled, pause, holding your breath for four seconds.
4. Then exhale, feel your abdomen contract, pushing your exhale out and make the exhale last four seconds.
5. Then, when you have exhaled, pause and hold for four seconds.
6. Repeat the process. Do this for a few minutes or 20 minutes. Whatever feels good for you.

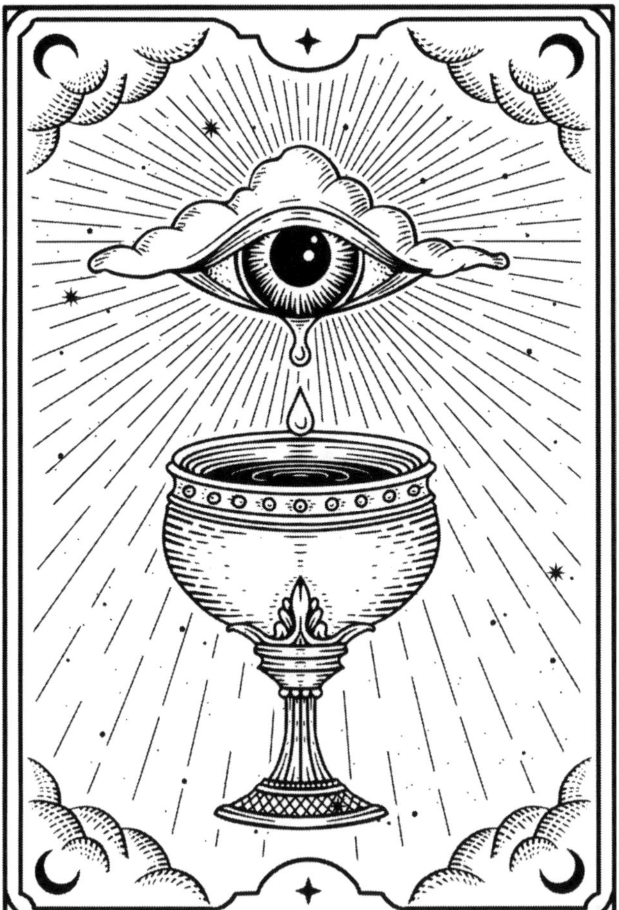

Altars

Altars have been in use since the beginning of human history. A stone carving of a God/dess placed on a piece of wood in a cave can be an altar, or a simple vase of flowers on a table alongside a picture can be an altar. They can be as simple or as elaborate as you wish.

One way humans experience Divinity is through creative expression. Artistic imagery, drawings, paintings, pictures, statues, etc. It feeds our human Soul. While we understand these are not the Divine itself, these images help us focus our attention on devotion.

The purpose of the altar is to inspire us to open our hearts and bring us into a state of Divine connection or reverence.

The altar starts with a flat surface, like a table or other piece of furniture on which to place sacred objects. It is imperative that you create an altar to support your spiritual journey if you do not already have one. It can be a tiny table in the corner of your bedroom or a whole room dedicated to your sacred time. Maybe you can easily find a place in your home for your sacred space—or you may have to be more creative.

There are many different kinds of altars, divided into two categories: personal and public.

A personal altar is what we are going to talk about here. This is an altar that is used for your spiritual practice.

Guidelines

+ Select somewhere that is private and that you love. Place it somewhere out of the way from others walking by it, if possible. Cover it with a black (preferably silk) cloth when not in use if there is a chance that other people's eyes will see it or other people will walk by it. It is very important that no one but you use it, look upon it, or touch the items that are on it because their psychic energy or vibration can affect the energy of your sacred items.
+ Gather items to place on it that have special meaning for you. A rock you found on a hike, a picture of a loved one, a necklace someone gave you. A crystal that has properties you need at this time. Anything that fills you with a spiritual feeling.

You can have more than one. I personally have several around my home. They can all have a different purpose, but the one I am asking you to protect from others is your personal sacred altar. You can have others set up in the home that can be shared.

Altar Supplies

Gather what resonates for you to create a feeling of love and Divine connection. Here are some suggestions:

+ Goddess symbol: Anything that represents Divine feminine for you.
+ God symbol: Anything that represents Divine masculine for you.
+ Knife: Only for ceremonial purposes. A black handle is best for this, but not required. You can use this to call in the directions and open your sacred space.
+ Wand: This can have many uses, like holding it during your meditation to focus or for drawing runes over your intentions you write before you burn them. One person even used an old key as this symbol because it felt right for her. Remember: it must feel good for you!
+ Censor: Incense holder/burner.
+ Devotion symbol: Pentacle, cross, ankh, etc.
+ Chalice: A cup, goblet, or bowl for water.

- + Bowl for salt: Can be a shell, pinch bowl, etc.
- + Incense
- + Flowers, greenery: Whatever the season's foliage is.
- + Fruit/food and offering plate: Offering of the season.
- + Candle: Color of season/festival or ritual.
- + Broom: Large or small handheld.

Cleansing Your Items

One of the important things to do as you set up your altar is to cleanse the items you gather before you place them on your altar. There are many ways to do this.

Here is the simplest:

Use an herb and burn it to smudge your items. "Smudge" means to light the herb and allow the smoke to cleanse/clear the items—and yourself—in the smoke. It transmutes negative energies. After cleansing them, you can place them on your altar.

Smudging Supplies

- + Herbs, woods, and resins that clear: Sage, Palo Santo, Frankincense, Myrrh, etc.
- + Feather or feather fan (optional) to move the smoke.
- + Shell or fireproof bowl to put the burning herb in.

Placement of Items

There are many different traditions - please use the traditions that feel right for you. If you have a love for the Virgin Mary, then she can be on your altar. If Ganesha is your guy, then use him! There are lots of different ways to create the altar.

What matters most is that when you sit before it, you feel LOVE.

Here are some suggestions for placement as you are facing your altar:

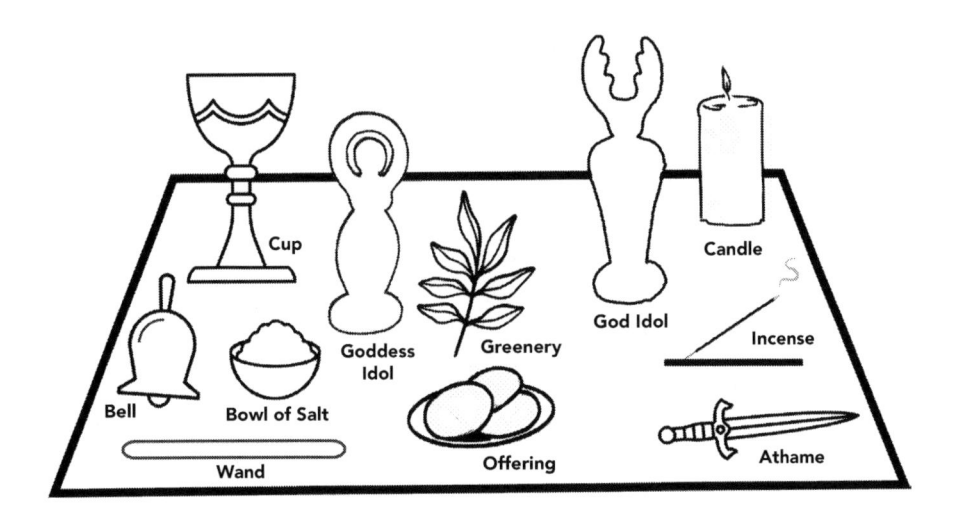

Altar diagram labels: Cup, Candle, Bell, Goddess Idol, Greenery, God Idol, Incense, Bowl of Salt, Offering, Athame, Wand

Using Your Altar

The altar is the place that creates a sense of sacredness for you. Have a set time each day, beginning or end of your day, and spend time in communion or devotion with the Divine.

As soon as you sit down, you should feel your body relax, your senses heighten, and a calm come over you. This will increase as you practice it.

Designate a block of time each day for this. It can be 10 minutes if that is all you have—or an hour if you feel it. At least 20 minutes once a day is highly recommended. Twice a day, before you start your day and again at the end of your day, is optimal.

Opening Sacred Space before sitting at your altar sets the energy for you to be in a protected environment so you may let your energy blossom and unfold to receive, free of any adverse influences. While you are in this sealed "container" doing your sacred work, you are building a powerful field of magic. All the beautiful intentions and creations fill up this container. The alchemy of what you are transmuting, building, and manifesting strengthens.

Once your work, intentions, and creations are fully complete, you are done with your session.

The energy you created in the beginning is very different than the energy that is alive by the time you finish. Because of this, all the pieces of your creation had time to transform within this alembic or cocoon. It was kept pure, clear, and aligned.

By the time you are done with your altar time and release your Sacred Space helpers or circle, your creation will be released into the world in its full embodiment, whole and complete. What you were able to create was much more powerful because you contained it until it was finished instead of leaking energy during the process. These are the reasons we create Sacred Space and use a magic circle.

Recap

In dissolution, you are letting the "old" fall away to make room for new openings, new beginnings, and new life to flow to you. In this phase, it is critically important to have a personal system and environment that you can go to for meditation, to sit at your altar, or go into ceremony to get the support, guidance, and help to recenter yourself. Having a daily practice—even when not going through a dissolution process—strengthens your Divine connection and Union.

Go Deeper

Here are some questions to contemplate during this stage:

Death (Ego death, small self, letting go)

The false self must die before the true self can be reborn.

+ What part of you or your life needs to be let go of? What no longer serves you?
+ What part needs to die because it is holding you back from experiencing the peace and freedom that your Soul seeks?

- What are the things in your life that you feel are holding you back from living the life you really want? Now, while looking at your answer, consider it differently. Ask yourself how you can start to give yourself those things now so you can change the frequency of your life and allow changes in your outside experience to align with your true inner desires.
- What part of you has been hiding deep in the Shadow because you do not want to look at it or acknowledge it?
- How can you sit in the Shadow and finally allow all of yourself to be seen, sit with all you have been and done, and say, "You belong. Let me see you." Send love and forgiveness to yourself and all those Shadow parts. Now, with forgiveness in your heart for yourself, what can you let go of, release, and surrender so you can be free?
- Moving forward, what will you do to live in freedom?

Know that nothing is ever lost. Death is not permanent, but just a transition. Nothing was ever not worth it, for it brought you to this very moment now.

Giving

What of yourself are you willing to offer up to the world?

- Who am I? Why am I here?
- What am I willing to give up to receive transformation and truth?
- What am I still holding back?
- Which areas of my life do I need to open up to assist others (people, animals, earth, etc.) more?
- What do I need to give to myself…FINALLY?

Inner Work/Spirituality

What aspects of your inner self are changing?

- What changes am I seeing?
- Which things are still stuck?

- Which aspects of myself or life still need to shift?
- What does this dedication to myself mean to me?
- What does God/dess mean to me now?

Childhood Dreams

What childhood aspects of yourself need to be remembered?

- Which aspects of your inner child are asking to be heard?
- What things were lost through the years that you now want to remember and acknowledge?
- Which aspects of you as a child need to be healed?
- In the most pure and innocent answer, what do you really want your life to be now?

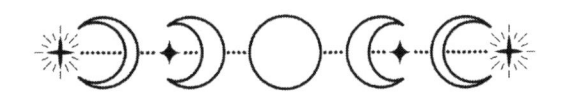

Transcending Time

To meet you whole within myself,
To meet my equal, my flame.

To transcend time and limitations,
This time with everything offered,
For us to move forth and become what we already are
but have only forgotten.

When I love you, I love myself,
When I give to you, I give to myself.

No separation,
we are all one.

In this place of purity, this place of innocence, this place of Unity
I give you all and
Ascend.

—Sarah Michelle Wergin

PART 2: PURIFICATION

Purification is the point when the light begins to do its work, clearing and cleansing everything it touches. It assists the process of change, transformation, and transmutation, and you will see the old being replaced by the new. This stage can be called Albedo or Sattva.

At this place in one's life, there is a sense of opening. You may still be feeling the complete uncertainty—and even fear—but you are in the process and are now sensing that letting go is all you can do. You are aware of what you need to release, integrate, or change. You are able to start to let go of things, people, situations, habits, and environments, and as you do this, you feel yourself and your life becoming lighter. You are clearing out the old. It could be as simple as decluttering your house or as complicated as getting a divorce—and everything in between.

This purification process can clear your emotions, but at the same time, you will have a new, fresh vibration coming into you. There can be a mix of excitement and sadness as you are still going through grieving the loss of the old.

Embrace it all.

You can be excited and grateful AND sad or angry—all at the same time. Every emotion belongs; whatever you are feeling is perfect. No judging! Just allowing! Surrender.

During the purification stage, you may start to remember things from your past in a new way. You may remember an activity you did as a child that you loved and want to connect to again. You can experience an aliveness coming back into you.

That is an indicator that you are in the process of purification. That sense of aliveness tells you your circuits are opening and clearing.

Life is meant to feel vibrant and alive. This is your signal to yourself that you are, indeed, on the right path! Do not let the signal go unnoticed! Pay attention.

This will be a trail marker that you are on the right path, finding your way back to your true self.

Pay attention. And then give thanks and be grateful at each instant that you feel good. Giving thanks and being in gratitude is how we expand more of that in our lives.

During playtime as children—without thinking—we often acted out the talents, skills, gifts, and purpose that we actually came here to have, do, and be!

As a kid, I always loved being in nature. I used to set up little kitchens in the forest and pick plants and grind them, pulse them with sticks, mix them, and act like I was creating a healing ointment or magical elixir. I knew there was so much about it that no one was telling me. I knew the plants did something, but I did not know what. Years later, becoming an herbalist finally showed me I knew what I was doing, even at the youngest age!

I also loved to play school with my little sister. Much to her dismay, I would create a class, make her sit there and listen, and then give her homework or assignments to do. I loved helping her learn. Decades later, teaching would become another one of my passions.

I was also deeply drawn to the mystical as a child, feeling, sensing, and knowing there was something more beyond what my eyes could see. Something magical that the mundane day-to-day existence of my family, school, and culture was just missing. It was a deep ache in my heart and Soul. All the superficial things just never quenched this thirst I felt inside for giving reverence to something more meaningful and, *actually, more real.*

Every day I just spent watching television or handing in an assignment at school lacked substance, purpose, and a greater understanding.

Years later, learning all I have about the esoteric arts, the occult, alchemy, magic, and spirituality proved to me that what I felt underneath the surface was right all along. I ended up creating a mystery school, teaching esoteric studies, and also leading sacred journeys to magical lands so people could remember that, YES!...the magic *is* real.

All these things I did as a kid, I felt as a kid, I *knew* as a kid...but I was just waiting until I was old enough to bring them into manifestation and embody them authentically. You can do this, too!

What things were you drawn to as a child? What truths did you know as a child? Remember back to those times and find those themes. They are clues about your gifts and your purpose.

During the stage of purification, you may be drawn to take up new hobbies, activities, or interests that are leading you back to your true Soul mission. This can be even more refined as you go into the stages of Rebirth and the Living Union.

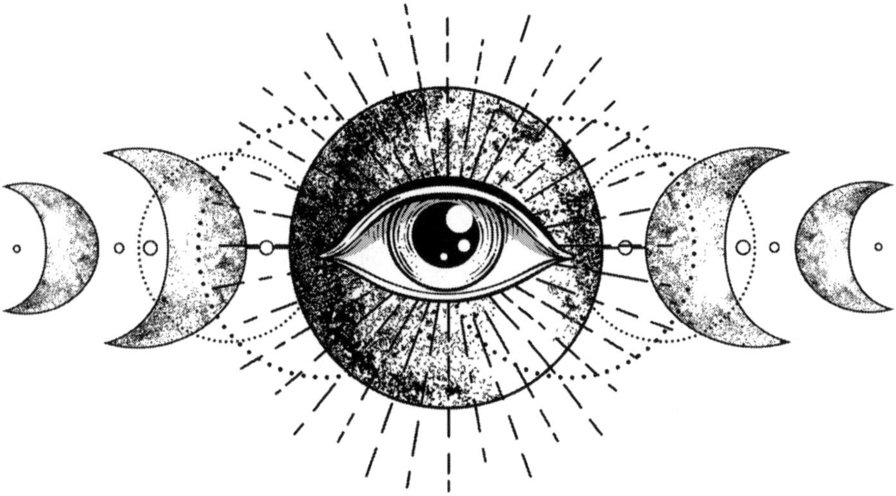

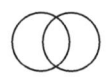

Transformation & Transmutation

Transformation is a change, an altered state of being. A bird learning to fly. Transmutation is a complete alteration from a lower state to a higher one. A caterpillar becoming a butterfly.

The Snake teaches transmutation, the alchemical art of taking something as it was given and changing it into something new. To do this, the old skin of what "is" must be shed. The process of taking density, darkness, and poison and transmuting it will turn what may be seen as a negative into gold, light, and medicine for your Soul.

Each bite you receive, each challenge in life you live through, each trauma you endure and persevere transmutes a part of you.

The initiation is the poison, the challenge, the pain. It can be undertaken on any level—mental, physical, emotional, or spiritual.

Two snakes entwined around the sword symbolize living illumination, the uniting of the masculine and feminine energies in each person, creating Divine Union.

Thoth the Atlantean, who later returned as Hermes and was the father of Alchemy, taught us this: Once you learn how to take the poison and transmute it, you shed the skin of your old self and are reborn into the next form of who you truly are.

By accepting all the aspects of yourself and your life, you surrender to the magnificence of the process and are illuminated. This is the significance of the Alchemical Fire.

Transformation comes from aligning your thoughts and using your mental capacity to adjust the energy with your emotional field. That begins the transformation. It can be challenging when we hold onto outdated beliefs. Some people hold on to them all their lives, and transformation is stuck or minimal. Others come to realize the process and embrace it.

Transformation leads to where your Soul is asking to go. Transmutation takes you to a higher level of conscious living.

Tools: Detox, Let Go, and Manage Your Energy

Humans have a way of complicating things, and never before has this been more true than right now. There is so much information, influence, and choices—more than ever before. And while some of these things can be helpful or beneficial, unfortunately, the majority of these choices have actually led people further away from what will birth their awakening and help them feel peace and happiness.

To realign, find your Soul path, and restore your health and well-being, you need to first return to the simple truths.

These ancient keys have been taught through every true spiritual practice. An early civilization—and a state of consciousness—Lemuria refers to these simple truths as "pillars." I call them the Five Pillars of Purity.

To find your way out of all the distortion and over-complication modern life throws in front of you, just start with the simple foundations. Return to these purities in your life, and then only add back in the things that feel right for you after that.

This is a way to help you realign, getting crystal-clear on what you need and what you do and do not want in your life going forward.

The Five Pillars of Purity

These areas, in balance, will lead to a pure mind, body, and soul.

1. Proper Breath

Breath is your first connection to life. Lungs are the ministers of the body. We eliminate 70% of waste from our body through our breath! How we breathe and the quality of the air we breathe is of the utmost importance.

Each day, practice taking deep breaths into the abdomen on the inhale, and then deeply exhaling, exhausting all the air in the lungs. Most people do not breathe properly for most of the day.

Our breath is connected to our emotions. When something unpleasant happens, it is common to hold our breath or start shallow breathing. It is a symptom of trying to hold in the trauma.

Another piece is that the lower chakras—the Root, Sacral, and Solar Plexus—all below the diaphragm, are where we hide the pain of these experiences and emotions. We push them down into those places so we can cope and not feel the pain of the emotion.

This process involves holding down or suppressing emotions, causing the body to breathe shallowly. When you consciously take deep breaths, the energy in the lower chakras seeks to rise. Activating your diaphragm might bring up uncomfortable sensations, revealing past, buried feelings.

As a child, your Sacral or second chakra, located about two inches below your belly button, is fully activated and utilized for powerful and pure creativity. It is in full force as a child. As you get to puberty, that chakra begins to channel the majority of that creative force into awakening sexual energy. It is at this time that most children start to become very self-conscious about their bodies. And they can begin pulling in their Sacral and Solar Plexus chakras because of this. It can be a protective mechanism, especially for girls.

When you are a child, you are carefree. You walk around with a nice rounded, free abdomen, not self-aware of how that looks or that there is anything wrong with exactly how your body is.

I can remember when this discord started for me. I was about nine or ten and was at camp one day when a boy made a comment to me that I had a big belly. Now, I was a thin kid. It had nothing to do with extra weight or anything. It was that I was just still walking around with my free, expanded Solar Plexus, fully confident in myself and my body.

At that moment, I became aware of my stomach. I remember consciously sucking it in. And I continued to do that the rest of my life until I learned otherwise because that was socially the norm. That experience planted a seed for me, to think that sucking in the stomach was what a girl should do or look like.

Painful or traumatic experiences also cause a person to suck in their breath and start shallow breathing. Any of these things become the unconscious process of the body wanting to protect itself from feeling pain. So it starts to suppress the breath—and can even reverse the cycle of the breath to reinforce this.

An example of this is how most people breathe the shallow and opposite way. They shallowly breathe by just raising their shoulders with each breath, as if letting the upper part of the torso do the breathing. They usually never really get a full breath down into the lower abdomen or stomach.

When you inhale, your lower abdomen should expand like you are blowing up a balloon. And when you exhale, that lower area should contract as you let out the air.

This is the opposite of what most people are doing! Try it yourself and see.

If you are breathing correctly, your shoulders do not move up and down. They stay still. It should all come from the abdomen.

I used to experience what doctors call "exercise-induced asthma." I would only experience trouble breathing when I exercised hard or went hiking, where I needed to breathe deeply. I would get very uncomfortable and feel like I couldn't breathe. I would even feel a tightness in my throat. I would feel many emotions coming up and would get anxious. I couldn't understand because there was no reason for them in that moment. I also had unresolved emotions that I had not dealt with from my childhood.

After I started doing deep spiritual work and clearing the wounding and trauma, I have never again experienced that when breathing hard or exercising.

As you start deep breathing, those emotions will try to rise into the upper chakras for clearing. It can feel overwhelming because these have been stuffed down for years or even decades.

Connecting breath to movement, like with Pranayama, Qi Gong, Tai Chi or Yoga, is such a healing process when just allowed to unfold. And proper breathing going forward will allow you to deal with emotions as you have them. Then you can become more aware, stay clearer, and detox your physical body as well as your emotional and mental bodies.

The other piece about breath to consider is the quality of your air.

It is imperative to do a thorough assessment of all the products you have in your home or space. The air in most homes is more toxic than the outside. Be committed to looking at everything you use in your home and on your body. Your skin is your largest organ, and everything you put on it gets absorbed into your systems. It is also considered an organ of the lungs in Chinese Medicine.

Make sure that every ingredient is natural and organic whenever possible. Check every cleaning product. There are so many brands of non-toxic cleaning products these days. But about 80% of the "natural" cleaning products still have some ingredients that can harm the body.

YOU MUST CHECK EVERY INGREDIENT!

Do not believe a product is non-toxic or all-natural just because it says it on the bottle. There is no regulation on using those words, and any company can make those statements without them being true.

Even if there is only a small percentage of chemicals in your product, those could be the endocrine disruptors or carcinogens that are creating an illness for you. Look up every ingredient on this website: www.ewg.org/skindeep/.

For these reasons, I personally make most of my cleaning products with simple ingredients—it's easy, effective, and inexpensive.

2. Proper Movement

Movement keeps energy flowing. Stagnation is where you will create disease. Energy, or Qi (chee), is what drives all the processes in our body. Getting enough of the right movement for your body type is imperative for keeping our bones, muscles, tendons, ligaments, organs, and skin healthy. It moves Qi and blood and keeps everything in our body in harmony. Move your body each day. Exercises like Tai Chi, Qi Gong, Yoga, Pilates, or the Five Tibetan Rites (stretches and poses that were used in Lemuria) all help move Qi.

5 Tibetan Rites

The level of intensity for exercise is dependent on your body type. One body type may thrive on intense endurance training; for another, it can weaken them over time.

Finding out what forms of exercise are best for you is important.

Just remember that daily movement moves oxygen, blood, and nutrients, and assists detoxification. This, in turn, assists all the organ systems to keep a body functioning optimally.

3. Proper Rest

Rest is just as important as exercise. When you feel like you need to rest, do not push through! Listen to your body and take some time to be still, whether it is a 10-minute break, a 20-minute nap, a week's vacation or a year off…respect what your body is saying. You will begin to heal and trust yourself again.

The still, quiet time you take allows for deep listening to the Soul. Your body heals when it rests, and by relaxing, it can detox and repair.

Most cultures in this modern age do not value rest enough. And it is quality rest that matters. Rest is not the same as being lazy. This is where you need to have awareness. Over-exercise is just as detrimental as not enough exercise. These are two sides of the same distortion coin.

Everything in balance.

It is critical to sleep the number of hours that is right for you. Everybody has the right number of hours of sleep that rejuvenates them. You can discover your optimal amount by doing this exercise several days in a row, like over a weekend or a vacation: As soon as you start to feel tired, allow yourself to go to bed. Do not do anything else. Just allow yourself to go to sleep and don't push through. Then, without an alarm and without any other distractions, what time does your body wake up? If you do this over time, you will see your rhythm. Find your perfect number of hours and arrange your life to give you that or as close as you possibly can.

I discovered this late in life. Had I discovered this sooner, my college years wouldn't have been full of adrenal fatigue! My optimal number of hours of sleep is nine hours. It doesn't matter what my activity level was in a day. This is because my body is highly sensitive and, because of all of the things that I experience, feel, and move through during the day, I need nine hours to completely discharge and regenerate. If I get less than that, I feel it. Even an hour.

Prioritize your sleep. Organize your life to go to bed at a certain time so you can fully recharge. You will have more energy and be less dependent on caffeine or other stimulants to get you through your day.

4. Proper Food and Drink

So much of what we have available to us is laden with chemicals. Eat clean food—as close to how Mother Nature created it as possible—and avoid artificial ingredients, preservatives, processed foods, microwaved foods, refined sugar, and other toxins.

Things in packages or that have been processed are going to be least desirable. Unfortunately, the system is set up so that these kinds of foods are the cheapest. If you're on a budget or low income, sometimes what food you can buy is dependent on this. But start making small changes in your life. You need to ask yourself this question first:

What are you setting up your life to support? What's actually going to bring you health, happiness, and harmony?

You need to eat, and what you put in your body will affect your mood, your attitude, and how you feel. And how you feel will affect your choices. Because our genes for digestion and what is "good food" for us actually sit on the genes that regulate emotions and moods, how you eat and what you put in your body affects your attitude towards life. It also will affect the kinds of emotions you have. You will have more anger, irritability, and frustration if you are nutrient-deficient. And the toxins created from the chemicals put a burden on the organs. If you are overloaded with candida from too much sugar, it makes it impossible for you to actually think and act clearly! These pathogens and compounds are so powerful. They actually can control you. And you need to recognize that.

If you need to change your whole life so that you can eat more cleanly, start with that.

I remember being a poor college student, working and paying for college, and having five dollars for the month to spend on anything. I would eat whole carrots as a snack. Not the fancy little finger knobs in a plastic bag, but a whole carrot with a green on top. That was my snack. The entire time, I was using organic skin care because that's what matters to me. I made my lunches ahead of time—organic beans and rice—and didn't go out to eat.

I made sure that I was using biodynamic organic skin care because I knew how important what I was putting on and into my body was. I absolutely found a way to make it all happen. I shopped for all my clothes in second-hand stores. I didn't go out and party on the weekends. I didn't go to the movies. I didn't do many of the things that some of my friends were doing. It was more important for me to really simplify my life. Take care of the things that would keep my body healthy. That way, I would have all of the energy and creativity I needed to learn, dream, and plan my future. And I didn't go into debt, which is a huge issue for many young people.

Don't spend more than what you're making. And make what you have work for you.

Eating organic and non-GMO foods and beverages is best. The unfortunate thing is even people eating the cleanest diets are still exposed to toxins in the environment. At this point on the planet, toxins are everywhere. There are nutrients and supplements that can help bind these toxins and eliminate them from your body. With so many brands and different companies now all having their own agenda, get support from a trained professional.

Ask yourself, with each item you are ingesting, "Does this promote life?" Everyone's body is different. There is no one diet that is right for everyone. Start listening to and feeling what your body tells you!

Stop the guilt and shame, and giving your power away to "experts." Listen to what your body tells you. Your body is like a tuning fork or antennae for the guidance of your Soul. The body will give you signals; you just need to listen to it.

To do this effectively, you must be clear. If you are full of toxicity, exhausted, over-stressed, and out of balance, what you may hear are the pathogens or toxins telling you what they need you to eat to keep feeding them, not what is actually good for your body.

If your body has been screaming at you, "I am toxic, exhausted, over-stressed, and out of balance," it is up to you to listen to it. Get clear so you can actually hear what it needs. Seek professional assistance when necessary.

By following these foundational steps, I guarantee that all your other endeavors will flow more smoothly, bringing greater fulfillment and aligning you with the life you truly desire. The key lies in feeling good, being happy, and maintaining your health. Skipping any of these essential aspects may result in a state of deficiency, escapism, and disappointment in your life.

5. Proper Thoughts

Become the watcher of your thoughts and learn to choose them, just as you would select seeds to plant in your garden. What you let your mind do and think all day will create your reality.

These are the seeds of creation! Choose, plant, and reap positivity.

This also takes time, and this is where you have to be dedicated. You have to make restructuring your internal habits a priority over mindless activities or any other things society might tell you you "should" do.

Having a gratitude practice and meditation is imperative. No matter what is happening in your life, you find the things you are grateful for every day. You do this morning and night and start giving thanks every time something good does happen to you. Then, these good things will start to grow more fully in your life.

But it's hard to feel gratitude when you feel sick, exhausted, or are living in a toxic environment or toxic relationships. So you have to be grateful for the things that are good and are working.

At a cellular core level, every human knows what a clear, pure existence feels like.

There is disruption or discord within most humans who are living with all the distortions around us. But drop anyone into a clean, clear, natural environment and they feel the difference. This is what you need to do. Clear out the "distortions" and then decide how to rearrange your life so this becomes your new normal.

You have to be the catalyst to create the shift.

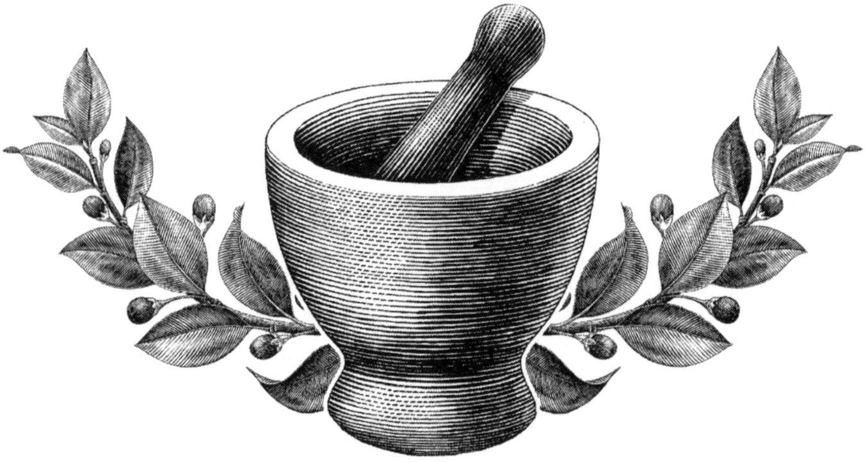

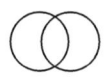

Detoxifying Your Body

The body is the temple for your Soul. A proper cleanse or purification of the body is an important act that should be done, at minimum, in the Spring and Fall seasons every year. You do it when the weather has warmed enough that your body understands it is time to "let go" and release. It should also be done when you are able to take the time for stillness and decreased activity, to allow the body to relax and focus on regeneration.

There are infinite ways to do a cleanse or purification ritual. The most important thing is that you are either fully educated on the process or you seek the guidance of a trained professional. Many methods out there are not sound and can make you sick when done without proper knowledge. Not everyone's body is ready for a fast, nor is everyone's constitution able to handle a juice cleanse! You need to know the state of your body to pick the correct path for you.

It is not appropriate to fast in the dead of winter, nor is it a wise idea to eat raw food if you are of a weak constitution! I believe each person's body has unique needs, and this should be honored. No diet or way of eating is right for every person. It is best to have a professional practitioner guide you.

The following are some guidelines to assist your process of purification:

+ Select a detox or cleanse and a time frame that is right for you and what you want to achieve—one which you will follow through and complete. Optimally, you will want time off from work and rigorous activity. It is a time to go inward, reflect, renew, and release toxins, past experiences, and "stuck" emotions. Do not be surprised if old thoughts or feelings rise to the surface—this is a part of the healing.

+ Take much of each day to sit quietly, meditate, or pray. Take naps and light walks in nature, and do light stretching, Yoga, Tai Chi, or Qi Gong. Take time to bathe in the sun, soaking up its healing rays (10-20 minutes daily) and do deep breathing.

If you are healthy and have the time to devote a day or more to being mindful and cleansing, then here are some guidelines. This sample cleanse can be done from one day to one week. If you choose to do more than five days, you should be under the supervision of a health practitioner.

+ Start the detox on the evening before day one. Let this meal be light—steamed vegetables are optimal. When you eat, let the focus be only on the food in front of you. Focus on your chewing, savor each bite, and notice all the different tastes that you are experiencing. Do not read or watch television while eating. The emotions you have while eating actually affect the frequency of the food and make it either medicine or poison for your body. Be mindful and intentional about nourishing your body. To start the digestive process in your mouth and to get the most out of your food, chew each bite 30-50 times. Stop eating when you are about 80% full.
+ Break a cleanse gradually or you may shock your system and undo all of the work you have done. The first day of breaking a cleanse, you may add back in more variety of fruit, veggies, whole grains, or legumes. By the second day, you can resume your normal diet.
+ If you are fasting, first add back fruit as a meal, then veggies as a meal, then legumes and grains, and lastly animal proteins.* Do this over a 36- to 48-hour period to allow for a gradual reintroduction.

I recommend that you eat foods that are in alignment with your blood type/genotype and that you do not have allergies or sensitivities to. Some people do not digest legumes well, and meat is healthier. And for some, it's the opposite. Pick your foods accordingly.

Daily Detox Drink & Cleansing Diet

- Pure/Filtered Water
- Lemon Juice
- Pure Maple Syrup (optional)
- Cayenne pepper
- Mung or Aduki Beans (sprouted best)
- Brown Rice or Millet (sprouted best)
- Kombu Seaweed
- Sea Salt
- Fruit: apples, pears, prunes or figs

Use all organic products. All of the above ingredients are recommended unless there is a known allergy to them.

WATER IS CRITICAL! Fresh spring water is best, then purified water—but remember that you need to add the minerals back in if you are doing reverse osmosis.

Daily Detox Drink

(to be used with a fast or with cleansing diet)

- 1 quart pure/filtered water
- 2 tbsp lemon juice—this flushes the liver
- 1 tbsp maple syrup (decrease, if needed)—this stabilizes the blood sugar and supplies trace minerals and B-vitamins
- 1/8 tsp cayenne pepper- this flushes the kidneys and blood

Combine the above ingredients. Drink all day, up to 2 quarts per day, to cleanse the liver, clear the kidneys, cleanse the blood, and maintain blood sugar levels.

Daily Cleansing Diet

Pre-Breakfast:

+ Start each day with warm lemon water. Pour 8 ounces warm water over 1-2 tbsp lemon juice (½ lemon). Add a little of the lemon zest/rind, as this has the bioflavonoids in it. Drink on an empty stomach.

Breakfast:

+ Sauté lightly with water and some selected fruits. You may use ghee if you have issues with hypoglycemia. You may add a touch of cinnamon or ginger if you like.

Lunch/Dinner:

+ Cook soaked/sprouted mung or aduki beans and grains (brown rice or millet).
+ Cook mung or aduki beans with kombu seaweed pieces to aid digestibility and detox process.
+ Lightly sauté or steam vegetables. No nightshades (peppers, eggplant, tomatoes, etc.) or root vegetables (potatoes, carrots, beets, onions, etc.).
+ Flavor with sea salt, if necessary. Eat small portions mindfully.

Note: If you are sensitive to phytic acid, you will need to alter this with vegetables only.

Other Detoxifying Foods

You may include the following foods in your diet and if you are unable to follow the above.

+ Black sesame seeds
+ Swiss Chard
+ Radishes/daikons
+ Beet Greens

- Turnips
- Dandelion Leaves
- Ghee (clarified butter)

Additional Add-Ins

- Wheatgrass/Barley Grass (1 oz juice 1-3 times daily, or take as directed in powder form)
- Blue-Green Algae: spirulina or chlorella (for cleansing and to decrease hunger; also found in tablet form)

Baths

Sea Salt baths are highly recommended to support detoxification: 1-2 cups per tub. I like Dead Sea Salts for the increased mineral content.

You can also do a Magnesium Flake bath: 1-2 cups per bath. Epsom salts are okay, too, but those are USP magnesium made in a laboratory.

Another addition is adding a box of baking soda to the bath, as this is a great way to detox from radiation exposure. I love to do this after I have traveled by airplane because we can get a lot of radiation exposure from that. Mustard seed powder can also be added, 1-2 tbsp to promote sweating and detox.

Do dry skin brushing (see diagram on next page) before you get into the bath to open the pores and assist the lymphatic system.

Make the bath hot and try and stay in for 12-20 minutes. Any longer than that and you actually can start to reabsorb the toxins.

DRY SKIN BRUSHING

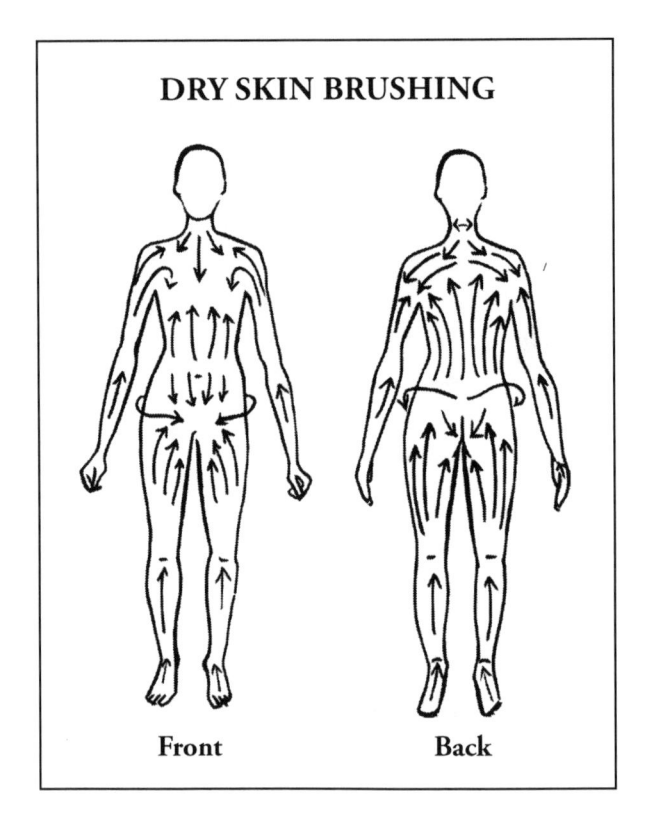

Front   Back

Laxatives

+ Dandelion Root (may be taken as a tea or in capsules)—1 tbsp dried root to 2 cups water, boil with lid for 20 minutes.
+ Ma Zi Ren Wan (Chinese formula)
+ Senna Leaves (Use sparingly and ONLY if dandelion root is not enough)

Note: It is very important to maintain regular bowel movements every day while on the program. This is one of the routes that the toxins can leave your body. You should be having at least two per day.

RECOMMENDED:

Purification Tea

This is a custom blend I make myself:

- 1 tbsp each: Red Clover flowers, Cleavers, Nettle leaves, Dandelion root, Horsetail, Rosemary, Yarrow, Echinacea, Blue Flag, Fennel seeds, Marigold flowers, Sage leaves, Sarsaparilla, Sassafras, Star Anise (whole), Basil
- Cloves (1 tbsp whole or 1 tsp dried ground)
- Ginger Root (1 tsp dried ground)
- Cayenne dried ground (¼ tsp)
- Cinnamon dried ground (¼ tsp)

Mix all ingredients in a bowl. Put in a jar and store in a cool, dry place.

Make an infusion: Pour 8 ounces boiling water over 1 tbsp of mixture and steep with cover for 20 min. You can drink this daily.

* Or make your own herbal blend

Note: You may experience flu-like symptoms, mental fogginess, or weakness. These are signs that toxins are leaving your body. If these symptoms become severe, consult a healthcare practitioner, as you may be detoxing too quickly.

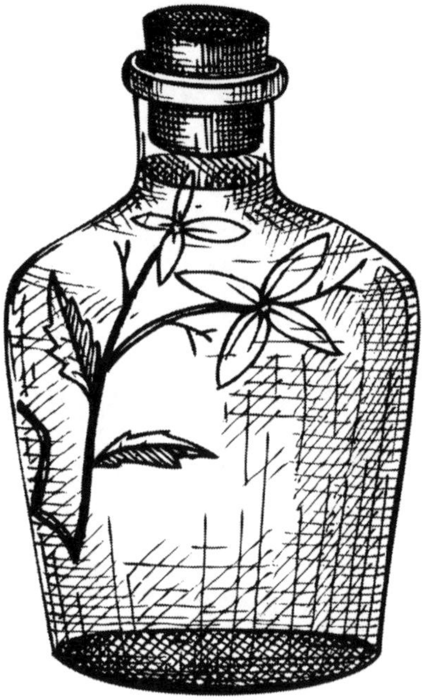

Detoxifying Your Life

If you get still enough, quiet enough, and clear enough you will see all the things you clutter your life with that you don't need or that are distractions.

These can just be pacifiers to make yourself feel better for a few moments or hours. Or they may actually be really toxic, keeping your body and mind in a state of overwhelm and making it harder to feel good and clear.

From the place of LOVE of self, LOVE of the other, LOVE of all life, LOVE of Creation…this is a time to start making new traditions, new habits, new memories…living truths that begin the dissolving of all thoughts and actions that keep life in a cycle of suffering.

You have the power to change it. And it starts with our daily, seasonal, and familial traditions.

By doing this, we bring the mystical into the practical.

Now, before you are ready to fully embrace the new energy, you must let go of the last remnants of the old and prepare your energetic field for the abundance of the vibration that is the NEW YOU that awaits!

This means cleansing your mind of unsupportive thoughts, purging outdated things, or releasing relationships in your life that are draining or toxic to you. To allow joy to fill us up, we need to CLEAR OUT the crap on every level to make room for the joy and light to flood in.

With this new vibration coming in, what doesn't feel right anymore?

Be an observer of your life. Pretend you are your most beloved friend who will always tell you the truth. Step outside yourself and see what you see.

As you change and grow, you will need different things and people to support you in the life you want to create. Just because something or someone is in your life now doesn't mean that they will serve your highest good in the future. Nor, if they have been in your life in the past, will they necessarily serve you now in the present. Remember that the energy goes both ways! You may not be their highest good anymore, either.

When you are living in alignment with your truth, you create the conditions for others to do the same. Discernment is key.

Doing clutter clearing, organizing, and purging of "stuff" is important for the purification phase. Clear out what you do not need. Throw it away or gift it to friends, family, thrift stores, etc. Sometimes it is hard to start this process, but once you experience how good it feels when finished, you will look forward to it each time.

What you clear on the outside will clear and open you inside. This is what Feng Shui is based on. Our environments are a reflection of our inner bodies/psyches. "As within, so without."

You have to let things go in order to make room for new, wonderful, beautiful, blissful things to come to you!

Ask yourself:

Do I use it? Do I need it? Do I love it?

If you use it (meaning you use it regularly), you can keep it.

If you need it, you may keep it.

If you love it, you can keep it.

But you can't keep 10 of them! If you have things you love, but have an excessive amount of them—such as ten pillows, and you love them all—you need to let go of most of them and only keep the one you love the most. An easier way to get started with this is to get rid of half. Then, on your next purge, cut that by half.

You will be amazed at how this practice makes room for more things you love to come to you—in every area of your life.

The Law of the Universe is that when you need to let go of something, there is someone else across town who may be praying for that exact thing to come into their life. You letting go of what is not a match for you anymore actually blesses someone else.

Crystal Basics

Our amazing Earth offers so much support to keep our bodies healthy and pure. Food and water are not the only things she creates for us—crystals are also here to support our wellness and evolution!

Crystals are densely manifested light. They are alive and grow and change, just as we do. They have a consciousness and are here to assist all life and the planet.

They all have their own jobs and gifts to share. Some are meant just to hold stillness and love far away inside the earth, unseen to all. Some are here to work with humans to help them on their ascension path. Some are here to record events, some to help others to travel to other dimensions. There are many reasons and purposes for them.

The subject of crystals is vast and infinite. Depending on who you ask, there will be different meanings for the same kind of crystal. There are some constants for the descriptions of classes of these stones, but the information from different crystal communicators can vary.

When working with crystals, you will find they are very loving, and the more time you spend with them, the easier it will be to understand them. You can actually tune into them and ask them what they are here for.

CLEAR QUARTZ

This is the most common and well-known of crystals. It can be used for many purposes. It represents the sum total of the material plane. With six sides, it symbolizes the sixth chakra, with the termination end being the seventh. They reflect pure white light and are made within the womb of the Earth. They show us perfected consciousness and will vibrate the aura at a high rate, helping dissolve and release the denser seeds. They can come in many colors and subcategories.

To introduce these into your life, here are some basics about the many types of clear quartz:

GENERATOR

Six-sided with single termination.
They can focus and direct energy. These range in size from the size of a grape to huge ones as big as a car. This type is here for radiating energy and holding clear space.

Helpful Use: Have one in the center of your home, radiating and holding light!

CLUSTERS

Many single-terminated crystals that share a common base.
Great for keeping an area to purify the energy or creating a magnified healing vibration. These are great for purifying and recharging other stones, crystals, or jewelry. Just lay them on the cluster for three or more hours.

Helpful Use: At night before bed, put the jewelry you have worn that day on the cluster overnight.

DOUBLE-TERMINATED

Six-sided with two terminations.

They can draw in or emanate energy from both sides. They are great for laying on the body to clear a chakra or organ and also to direct a chakra to spin in the correct direction. These are more rare than generators.

Helpful Use: Use to square off and ground the energy of a "missing" gua of your home according to Feng Shui (see below).

TABULAR

Flatter quartz with two of the opposing sides having a wider & larger surface.

They have a very special, high vibration. Great for telepathy and also powerful for emotional balancing and communication with your Higher Self. These crystals are wonderful at supporting a person going through intense mental and emotional issues.

Helpful Use: During a really emotional time, lay one on your Heart or Solar Plexus chakra and ask it to help you recenter and regain peace.

RECORD KEEPER

They have one or more sacred symbols engraved on one of their facets.

These shapes are not easily seen and will need to be sought out. If it is a true Record Keeper, it will carry one or more small perfect triangles on one of the six faces forming the termination. It will look like It Is etched Into the crystal. You will feel the indentation if you run your finger over it. This is an ancient universal symbol representing the trinity, which is Divine Union: you are in alignment with the God/dess aspect of creation. It is the portal of the crystal and the doorway into powerful wisdom. If you find one, it is a great responsibility to use it purely. It has the job of holding ancient knowledge and wisdom and was meant to return to bestow this upon the person with a pure heart.

Helpful Use: Have your Record Keeper in your office or on your altar so it can transmit messages and ideas to you that will assist you on your Soul path.

PROJECTOR

These can be several kinds of quartz. The qualifier is the termination/or terminations must be pointing out in the same direction from a flat base.

They are ideal for use in programming because they send out thoughts and images that are transferred into them.

Helpful Use: Great to use when you have an idea that you want to send into the Universe for manifestation. Sit in meditation, formulate your thoughts clearly, hold it between your hands at your Heart chakra, or put it to your forehead and think about the message clearly.

BALLS

Possess the power of seeing into the past or future.

Used by the trained to see and know. If you use them for this purpose, it is best to keep them covered and away from other eyes when you are not using them.

Helpful Use: Have one on your altar that radiates guidance during your ceremonies.

PHANTOM

These have smaller pyramid crystals inside the crystal.

They have undergone evolution of their own and can unlock secrets in your own Soul. The enlightened beings from far away that first inhabited our Earth stored ancient knowledge in them—galaxies of knowledge—in these special crystals so that when the time was right on the planet, they would rise to the surface for our use. These can be a trusted ally In your spiritual evolution.

Helpful Use: Keep one by your bedside to connect to during your sleep.

LASER WAND

Long and slender shape with small facets comprising the termination, and it tapers from base to point, with the base being wider.

These were once used in the healing temples of Lemuria, and with meditation, you can discover how to heal with them, such as energy "surgery." They can be used to create a protective field or also communicate with other worlds.

Helpful Use: Use it on yourself by sweeping it over your aura in any area where you feel the need to cut a cord or attachment to someone.

TRANSMITTER

Configuration of two symmetrical seven-sided faces with a perfect triangle located between them.

One can connect to the highest wisdom and receive truth necessary for one's growth to enlightenment. Can also use it to program and ask questions.

Helpful Use: When in sacred space, meditate with this crystal and ask for the truth of a situation or guidance on the next steps to take on your path.

WINDOW

Presence of a diamond-shape located on one side, such that the top point of the diamond connects with a line that leads directly to the termination.

They are the teachers, opening windows for one to see beyond the illusionary realm into the essence of the Self.

Helpful Use: Place on your altar to help you see beyond this reality or on your bedside table to help you access higher realms during sleep.

TWIN

The growing together of two or more crystals that are in parallel alignment.

Build relationships on all levels. Universal, group love.

Helpful Use: Use it in a group circle to hold the space and connect all participants.

TRANS-CHANNELER

Three, seven-sided faces, with a three-sided triangle face between them.

A continuous connective force of heart love between the holder and Source of All That Is.

Helpful Use: My favorite crystal to have on each window sill in my home and office.

CHANNELER

A seven-sided face located in the center front position of the terminated end of the crystal, a triangular face is located on the opposite side.

Access to innate wisdom of inner worlds and outer worlds. Can be used in meditation by asking specific questions or in combination with Record Keepers.

Helpful Use: Wonderful for your altar when you write out intentions or questions. Put the writing underneath it and wait for a cycle of the Moon to receive your information or guidance.

CROSS

This is recognized by an actual quartz formation in the shape of a cross on the crystal.

Powerful to assist in the removal of unwanted or other-worldly implants.

Helpful Use: Place this piece on the area of the body where the entity is attached or where you are having discomfort. Rest with it there for 20 min.

ELESTIAL

Natural terminations and etchings or layers all over the crystal.

Called the "Enchanted" crystal. When you see them, they feel like long-lost friends and have so much love and gentleness for us. Make no mistake, they are very powerful to help you transition from one stage to the next. They can help a soul clear wounds, burdens, or traumas.

Helpful Use: During your big energy shifts, up-leveling, or transformational periods, carry it with you during the day, sleep with it under your pillow, meditate with it, or place it on your altar. Also a great crystal for healers to have in the healing room to assist with treatments.

While white quartz is the most versatile, here are five other crystals that can support you:

+ **Rose Quartz:** Assists self-love and compassion, healing wounds around love.
+ **Amethyst:** An overall healing stone that can heal the mind, body, and Soul.
+ **Shungite:** Great to put near all your electronics, computers, cell phones, etc. It will help your body not be bombarded by the constant electromagnetic fields (EMFs) and allow you to become more able to sense subtle energies.
+ **Kyanite:** A gentle opener that aligns all your chakras and connects you to your Higher Self.
+ **Citrine:** A powerful yet gentle stone to clear any blocks to manifestation and abundance of all kinds. It can heal your center of free will, restoring your self-trust.

Practice these ways to use crystals:

Intentional purposes: Use them according to the kind of crystal they are, as listed above. After a crystal has been cleansed (see below), you are able to "charge" it with an intention, creating a partnership with it, asking it for what you would like help with.

Holding clear space: They can be put in any room to help keep the energy clear and pure.

Protection for the body and home: You can wear it as jewelry to keep you clear and also to purify your aura. You can just carry it in your pocket, as well. For protection against electromagnetic fields (EMFs), you can put one large or several small pieces (or Black Tourmaline or Shungite) around things like your computer, furnace, outlets, Wi-Fi, etc.

Support in your workspace (or altar): Keeping one on your altar, your desk, or your workspace is perfect for those that are with you to help with your work. It is a fun and magical experience to search out the crystals that are meant to work with you. When you are drawn to a crystal or one is given to you, you are meant to be together, for however long it is necessary. Always clear it first. Then, begin the process of finding out how it wants to help you.

Using crystals as jewelry or carrying them with you for a specific purpose: Just as with protection, this can be that you find different kinds of crystals that you want to work with. This could mean you are drawn to wearing citrine to help you vibrate with attracting abundance. Or you are drawn to wear carnelian to help you stay grounded and give you courage. The options are endless…do what feels good!

Personal healing layouts: This practice can be as simple as just putting the crystals you are drawn to upon your body where you are guided to do so. This could go as in-depth as you studying all the types of crystals and specific crystal patterns. It can be as simple as using what you have, such as a clear quartz on any chakra or part of your body where you are sensing imbalance. You can use this technique on others, as well as plants and animals. Place the quartz where you sense imbalance and allow the innate healing of the stone to do the work. Remember to always cleanse it afterward.

Cleansing Your Crystals

Always remember to cleanse your crystals regularly to clear out the negative energy that has accumulated. You can do this by…

+ Running it under cold water for one minute or more (faucet or even a creek, if you have access to one) and recharging it by putting it in the Sun for three or more hours. Make sure it is not a crystal that can fade in the UV rays, like rose quartz, amethyst, fluorite, or citrine.
+ Putting it out on the Full Moon overnight to cleanse and charge.
+ Using singing or crystal bowls: Put the crystal inside and play the bowl for one or more minutes.
+ Smudging them with white sage.

Feng Shui

Classical Feng Shui is an ancient art and science developed more than 4,000 years ago in China. "Feng" (pronounced "fung") means Wind, and "Shui" (pronounced "sh-way") means Water. In Chinese culture, gentle wind and clear water are associated with good health and good harvest.

Feng Shui is a complex body of knowledge that reveals how to balance the energies of any space to assure the health, harmony, and good fortune for the people inhabiting it.

This ancient art helps create a harmonious flow of Qi (pronounced "chee") throughout our living spaces or land. And, because all energy is affected by what is around it, our bodies reflect the flow of Qi in our environments—and vice versa.

Classical Feng Shui is set apart from other forms of Feng Shui as it goes very deep into the energies of each dwelling and the specific people living or working there. It combines the Chinese astrological information of the dwelling, a compass reading, and the astrological information of the people inhabiting the space.

Feng Shui for a home, business, or property is like acupuncture for the body and mind. It reads the elemental properties, discovers where the imbalances are, and then uses "remedies" to move the Qi, regulating and harmonizing the environment.

By looking at your body/mind wellness, you can see where you need support. Then, by looking at the energy flow in your home and business, you connect the areas that are affecting your body/mind, as well. Looking at these things together, you are addressing your whole life experience. That is how true healing takes place and is maintained.

This facilitates a complete energy shift, inside and out, because our internal state affects how we organize our environment…and our environment affects how we operate in our lives.

A perfect example of this is clutter. Clutter in your environment will cause clutter in your mind, affecting your mood and mental health, as well as your body, over time.

When you clear clutter or go through a purging of things, it can be very emotional. You are releasing memories, experiences, and feelings through that process. When you let things go, you also let a lot of the past go, too, and this can heal you on many levels. It allows for energetic pathways to be open so that new things, experiences, and people can come into your life. Open the pathways for Qi, and movement will follow.

If you feel stuck in your life, one of the easiest things you can do to get something moving is to rearrange your furniture or clean out clutter. Watch how your life changes.

Saltwater Cure

Saltwater cures are used to remedy the negative or inauspicious energies that are coming into a space from certain directions each year. The direction that these energies come in changes every year.

We start with the BaGua. This is the eight directions plus a center that makes up equal parts of your house or office. You lay this over your space, and you can see how each part of your home or office is divided up into the directions. You place a "cure" in the areas of the home or office to shift the energy.

The Chinese New Year begins on a different date every year, depending on the Lunar calendar and when the second New Moon occurs after the Winter Solstice. But the Chinese Feng Shui calendar shifts energy to the New Year on approximately February 4th each year. This day is called the Start of Spring, which is the date when the sun enters the 315th degree on the tropical zodiac. This is the most auspicious day to create your saltwater cures.

The areas (or "guas") that need a saltwater cure change every year. Having a Classical Feng Shui consultation can give you that information. Overall, having one in an area of your space that feels dark, negative, heavy, depressing, or stagnant is a good idea.

BaGua Map

Northwest Helpful People Travel	**North** Career Life's Journey	**Northeast** Knowledge Self-cultivation Meditation Wisdom
West Creativity Children Fertility Inner Child	**Center** Health Unity Wellness	**East** Family Community
Southwest Love Marriage Relationships	**South** How you share your light in the world	**Southeast** Wealth Prosperity

Supplies to make your own saltwater cure:

+ Salt (ideally high-quality coarse sea salt)
+ One container (glass or porcelain, not metal)
+ Six Chinese coins or a money coin/penny (must be made with copper—it is the copper that matters here)
+ Water (distilled or spring water to fill 3/4 of your chosen container)
+ A protective mat, cloth, or a stand.

Before you begin, it is best to center yourself with meditation, prayer, or just gentle breaths. Be mindful and get clear on your intentions for the cure, which should be to cleanse any negative energy from the space. Think it, see it, breathe it, and feel it. When you feel clear, create the cures.

Step 1: Fill your chosen container with salt up to ½ to ¾ of its capacity.

Step 2: Place the six coins on top of the salt in a clockwise circle. The coins should be placed with the Yang side up—the side with the four Chinese characters or the tail side of a penny.

Step 3: Add water to fill the container to the top or at least two inches above the salt.

Step 4: Place the container on a protective mat, cloth, or on a stand in the home area where you most need it.

Step 5: The saltwater cure container should be left open. Do not cover it or place it in a covered space, such as a kitchen cupboard.

Place your saltwater cure in an area where you know the container will be safe, meaning it will not be tipped over, moved, or otherwise tampered with. Usually, a room corner works well.

If you do not like the look of the saltwater cure, you can place it behind a decorative object so that it is not visible. For example, you can have your salt water cure behind the sofa, a screen, or a big, lush plant.

You should be able to have easy access to it, so you can add water and top it off when needed. But you do not want to move it if possible. It is said to disturb the negative Qi. Some traditions even use gloves to touch the container. Do not disturb or bump it!

Because the Feng Shui saltwater cure will absorb and accumulate a lot of negative energy, care should be taken with its disposal. Do not cleanse the bowl and the coins, but rather properly discard the whole cure. If you want to recycle, then take the coins and glass and recycle them in your bin—but never reuse them.

In some homes, this cure needs to be replaced every couple of months. In other homes, just once a year is enough. Keep an eye on your saltwater cure. As the cure absorbs negative energy, the salt can crystallize out of the water and grow over the container. If it looks like it has done a lot of work and the salt growth has left no room for water, then replace it with a new one. Otherwise, just keep topping off with water when needed.

Each Feng Shui New Year, you should throw your old coins, glass, and water/salt away. Because they store so much negative energy, it is best to throw them straight into the bin outside, if possible. Or, being mindful of the environment, you could gently take the whole cure and wash the salt outside into the earth—away from your garden—and recycle the glass and coins. But be very careful, and your intention and prayers will go a long way.

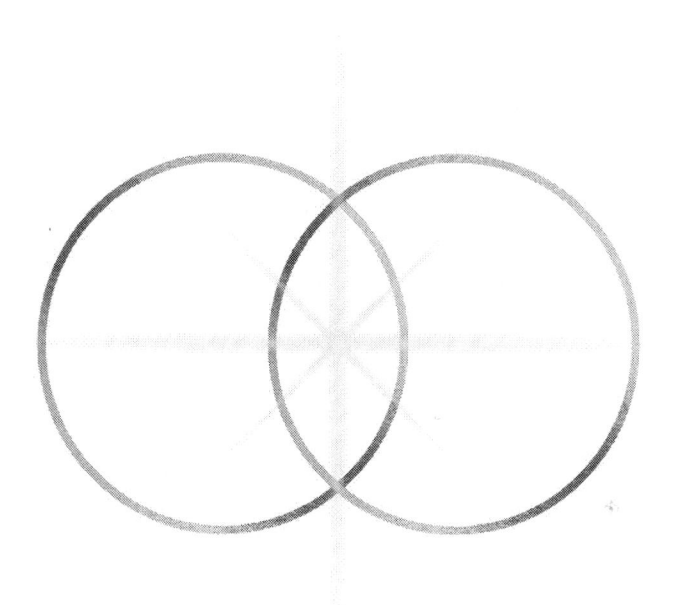

Cleansing Self & Others

Smudging the body is an ancient ritual used to purify the physical body and the energy body. It is important to do this often and with great intention.

As you raise your vibration and ascend, you become a brighter beacon of Light and Love. This state makes you more desirable to lower vibrational energies. You are a bright flame and very attractive to those forces. This is just a fact and needs to be acknowledged.

Take care to protect yourself, your home, your ceremony etc. Not from a state of fear but of empowerment. You need to become more and more diligent at watching your thoughts and actions so that they are in an empowered state, and in this frequency, you are protected and lesser energies cannot influence you.

Start making conscious choices to ignore the negative when it comes into your reality. Find the positive aspect of what is happening and refocus your attention on that! I like to remind myself, "Look at this through the lens of beauty!"

The most important thing you can do to clear yourself is to ask for Divine support, then do your clearing and protection, and know and believe you are protected.

If you live in fear and worry about negative energies, talk about them and think about them, you can give them more power. We all know people like this. If you have experienced this yourself, understand that a lower vibrational thought or emotion is the perfect entry point for more of that frequency to enter your life.

As soon as you turn toward the light, focus on love, and think and speak light, the Law of Attraction brings you that. If you are experiencing a strong dark/evil force, you may need to pick one of your "big sword" tools and do a ceremony or another energy practice with this. Here are a few that can help. Sometimes, professional help to get rid of it might be what you need.

Forgiveness is the most powerful clearing agent.

When you use it, you become a lightworker and are able to transmute any darkness by non-engagement in fear and invoking love.

The Hawaiian technique of Ho'oponopono is a great example of this. You just state in your mind: "I love you. I am sorry. Please forgive me. Thank you." Over and over. You are saying to the "other" but really to yourself. It calms the energy and cleans the energy up on the Universal plane.

Another one of my favorites is from Sanaya Roman's book, *Soul Love:* do a Soul Link. If there is toxic energy coming to you from someone else, you don't want to send love or light to that person because that personality may not be able to receive such a high frequency. It could actually make things worse because the vibe they will feel will be agitating to them. By connecting to their Soul, you are reaching the part of them that is above the persona and in a state of Divine love.

You link with your Soul by bringing your awareness from your body up above your head to a ball of light there. Feel it just by seeing or setting an intention that you are doing it. See or feel this light come down into your heart chakra and feel a sense of love, light, or peace. Breathe with this.

Now, bring your awareness from your heart chakra up to your head and above it to your Soul level again. From that level, have the intention to send love or peace to that person's Soul above their heads.

If, for some reason, you feel resistance, it could be your own or theirs, stop. It just means it is not the right time yet to try this. But if you feel ease, then just stay with the resonance of Divine Love and Light and see and feel your Soul sending it to their Soul.

You will feel the energy calm and become peaceful and soothing within yourself. In this state, say the things in your mind that you want to say from a place of love, such as, "I love you, and I release the tension or conflict between us. I am dedicated to finding a solution of peace for us." Or say, "I release you from playing this role for me. Go in peace." Or, "I realize we are both hurting. I forgive you and myself for the pain."

Just breathe and see and feel the love and light flow between you. Once you reach a state of calm, you can release the process.

Smudging (clearing with smoke)

White Sage, Palo Santo, Frankincense, and Myrrh resins or other herbs can clear your aura.

Tools:

+ Herbs for burning
+ Abalone shell or other fireproof container
+ Feather fan (or single feather) to move the smoke

Immersing yourself in the smoke or moving the smoke around your body actually dissipates negative energy and clears you. It sends it all back to Source for transmutation, and it is instant.

Directions:

+ Light the herb in a container and blow on it to get it to burn.
+ Once lit, use the feather or fan to move the incense and air. Start with yourself and gently breathe in a little of the smoke if you tolerate this.
+ Then hold the shell of the burning herb under you, starting at your feet, and move it up your body with arms out.
+ Do this front and back and stop longer in any areas that feel more congested.
+ When you are clear, you are ready to smudge others. You can also use toning, chanting, singing, etc., with this if you choose.

Water

You can purify with baths using sea salt, essential oils, flower essences, and herbs. Water represents Spirit, and salt represents the Earth. The electrical and ionic qualities of water and salt are very powerful and affect every cell in our body, as we are made of these elements.

Together, they invoke Spirit and Earth (Heaven and Earth) and create an open current in you to let go of anything less than love and then allow the Divine to flow freely into you. The essential oil, flower essence, or herbs you use carry properties as well, so pick them carefully.

Moonbathing/Sunbathing

The Moon and the Sun are powerful cleansers. Sitting out under the moonlight, or even being indoors and laying in the moonlight from a window, will clear your being.

Sunbathing, on the other hand, has become a polarizing topic.

In this day and age, exposure to the Sun has become looked upon unfavorably and is portrayed as dangerous. Yes, it is true that our atmosphere is not what it used to be, and we are responsible for the destruction of our protective barrier, but the Sun represents so much more.

The Sun is consciousness. The ancients used to do Sun worship, facing the Sun and taking in the rays through their eyelids and skin. Think of this metaphor: How many people walk around every day with sunglasses on and rarely allow the rays to be absorbed into their pineal gland? It mirrors the desire to keep people unconscious so they walk around just "obeying" whatever it is they are fed through media, political, or societal streams.

Soaking in the Sun's rays through the skin is imperative to good health, helping us synthesize vitamin D, one of the most critical nutrients in our bodies to fight disease, boost the immune system, and actually fight cancer! You need only 10-20 minutes per day of sunlight on your skin without sunscreen—the way nature created you to synthesize this.

Most people are so deficient in this nutrient because they don't spend enough time outdoors, in nature. Allow the rays to fall upon your skin, your face, and your eyelids. This pure light is connected to our consciousness, to life, to creation through our solar Sun, then through the great central Sun, and all the way to Source. This is a vast topic, but it is enough to say when you soak up the Sun's rays, you are soaking up pure love and light—as well as increasing good-mood hormones, immune-fighting nutrients, and awakening your consciousness!

So, on that note, I recommend that you develop a new relationship with the Sun, if you haven't already—one of hope, love, and consciousness.

Other Forms of Cleansing

+ Crystals (see page 119)
+ Sound: voice, bells, singing bowls, tingshaws, rattles, etc.

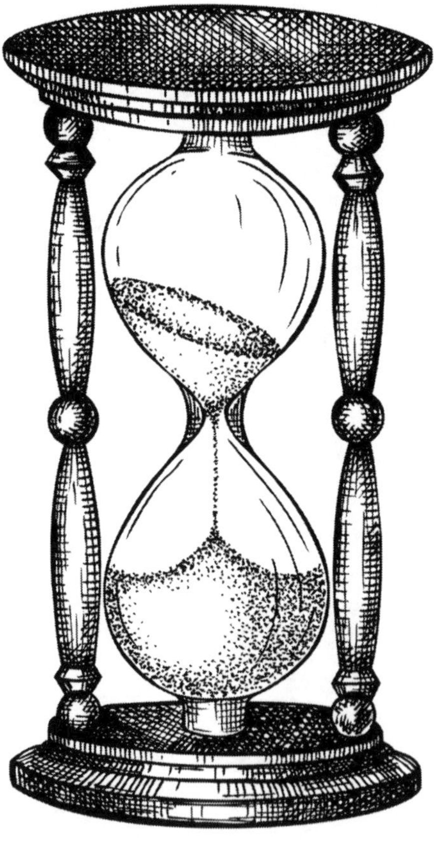

Managing Your Energy: Grounding, Clearing, and Protection

As you move through the purification process, grounding, clearing, and protecting your energy are imperative.

For the purification process to be effective on all levels, you must stay grounded. Grounding allows all the old emotions being cleared to effectively move out of your system. If you are not grounded, the energies cannot discharge properly and can get stuck in the body or field, or can cause the consciousness to become unstable.

Regular grounding will ensure there is an open connection between your upper chakras and lower chakras and that they are all getting the support they need. Also, the energy can freely move up and out and also down and transmute.

We are the connection between Heaven and Earth and are meant to be connected as a circuit flowing freely. If you spend too much time in the upper realms without grounding the energy, you can become unstable and not be able to function on the material plane well. This can affect your mental, emotional, or physical health.

Clearing is the process of letting go, releasing, integrating, or transmuting energies that are less than Divine Love, Light, and Truth. These energies or experiences create emotional vibrations that can get stuck in the bodies (emotional, mental, physical, etc.), and clearing is the process in which we allow them to come to the light and be transformed. This process purifies them.

Protection is critical when going through this purification process. This ensures that the lower frequencies that are getting released do not attract more energy of the same (or even lower) vibrational energies that can ride into the experience on the lower vibration and enter a person's field. Lower vibrational entities thrive on these frequencies, and it is how they are able to get into a person's psyche or body.

Grounding

Grounding does not mean that you are just connecting with the Earth or anchoring energy from above. Being grounded now means that you're checking to make sure that your energy axis, the energy that runs from your feet to your crown and vice versa—your axis mundi, up and down your spinal column—is open, clear, and flowing.

Many people and some traditions over-emphasize the "higher" chakras, meaning the ones above the diaphragm. They do this because they have a misunderstood belief that those are more righteous, important, significant energy centers. WRONG. They are all equal—and all need to be in balance with each other. It is common when awakening to put too much focus on these. Meanwhile, the lower chakras become out of balance.

Tending to the clearing, radiance, and vitality of ALL the chakras is how you open the higher chakras even more. For example, moving the dense energy of pain from your solar plexus up will cause your heart chakra to expand and become more vibrant.

A key to your self-realization and ascension is the harmonizing of all chakras, making sure your lower chakras are fed as much light as your upper chakras. This means you are a clear vessel.

Clearing

Take responsibility for your life experience! Keep yourself clear daily, and anytime you feel not quite yourself!

- **Smudge** with smoke or spray (see page 137).
- **Bath/Shower:** Use Sea Salt plus essential oils or flower essences or herbs (see page 113).
- **Chakra clearing in the shower or bath:** Clear and balance by moving your right hand over them counterclockwise (imagine there is a face of a clock on the front of you facing out) to clear. Starting with the center of your hands first, then bottoms of your feet, then go up your body chakras, spinning them just above your body. Rinse your hands in the water. Then recharge them clockwise by first imagining grabbing light from above your head and then go through each chakra as you did before, but this time spin the chakra with your hands clockwise.
- **Ceremony:** Lay or rub black obsidian, black tourmaline, or shungite on the body; do sound healing with tuning forks, Tibetan singing bowls, crystal bowls, chanting, or toning.
- **Earthing:** Put your bare feet on the earth (30-45 minutes/day, minimum). Your body does an ion exchange and discharges energy into the Earth, and receives healing and beneficial ions in return.
- **Herbs:** You can use these herbs for making an infusion (which is like making a tea): 1 tsp dried leaves/flowers or 2 tsp fresh leaves/flowers into a mug and pour boiling water over them. Steep for 10-15 minutes. Good ones for this include Basil, Cloves (use just a few whole or only 1/4 tsp ground), Juniper (use just a few whole or ¼ tsp ground), Rose Petals, Nasturtium, Parsley, Peppermint, Lemon Balm, Lemongrass. Or you can put these in your bath—throw a handful of leaves or flowers in the tub or put them in a cotton/gauze bag and put it in the tub, which is easier to clean.
- **Flower Essences:** Add 4-7 drops to your bath, put 8-10 drops in a spray bottle, and make a space or aura spray. Spray yourself three or more times a day. Rub a few drops on your solar plexus or whatever area feels imbalanced. Take 4-7 drops under your tongue or in water. Good ones for this: Yarrow, Rose, Geranium, Nasturtium (for more info, see Resources page).

+ **Essential Oils:** Add a few drops to your bath water or make a body spray with 8-10 drops in a spray bottle and spray your aura three times per day. Or add a couple drops to a carrier oil like Jojoba or Sweet Almond Oil and rub on the body. Good ones for this include Lemon, Lemon Balm, Lilac, Lime, Orange, Pine, Tulip, Rose, and Vetivert. Spikenard is great to rub on the bottoms of feet before bed, during times of transformation or stress.

Essential Oils

A few of my top favorites for magical purposes either on your spells/prayer sheets, topical anointing, or aura/room spray.

HEALING/HEALTH

Frankincense, Lavender, Lemon, Eucalyptus, Clove, Myrrh, Mint, *Pine

HAPPINESS/JOY

Lemon Balm, *Ylang Ylang, Neroli, Bergamot, Apple, Orange, Sweet Pea, Water Lily

LOVE

Frangipani/Plumeria, Rose, Sandalwood, Gardenia, Jasmine, Vanilla, Rosemary, Carnation

PROSPERITY/MONEY

Patchouli, Ginger, Lemon Balm, Oak Moss, Sage, Vetivert, Cinnamon

PROTECTION/PURIFICATION

Spikenard, Rose, *Yarrow, Angelica, Mint, Rosemary, Vetivert, Lemon, Clove, Geranium, *Pine, *Sage, *Camphor

Use in small amounts, diluted, and only topically if not sensitive/allergic.

**All above recommendations are being suggested for topical use only and if you are sensitive/allergic, use at your own discretion.*

Making a Flower Essence

Supplies:

+ Small glass bowl (the size will be determined by the flowers used)
+ Small glass jar with lid for storage
+ Fine mesh strainer
+ Tweezers
+ Scissors
+ Spring Water (distilled is ok if you do not have spring water)
+ Organic alcohol or distilled white vinegar.

Before you begin:

+ Cleanse all your supplies by smudging them or using another method to purify your tools.
+ Picking the best day that you will collect your flowers is important. You will want to plan ahead. The flowers are best collected when they are still fresh with morning dew. The dew carries a magical charge from the moon and stars overnight, as well as the charge of otherworldly energies that come through at the times of day the veil thins, which is the sunrise and sunset. You will want to have 4 hours of clear sunlight in the morning right after you cut the flowers. If you are making a moon essence, then choose a Full Moon night and do this process starting at sundown.
+ Choosing your flowers. Meditate on which flower you wish to make the essence with. Connecting to the spirit of the plant and what qualities you desire to work with will help you choose your flower. Once you know which flower you would like, take a moment to ask permission to use these flowers. This is medicine for the body, mind and soul, and how you collect the flowers sets the intentions for the frequency of the essence. Once you get permission, then listen to any messages the plant has to share with you, honoring its gift.

Collecting the flowers:

+ Before you begin this step, it is important to get centered and clear. Be mindful during this whole process, thinking positive thoughts, speaking prayers, toning, or chanting mantras to keep your mind focused and clear.
+ Once you have decided on which plant you are working with, take the bowl and fill it with spring water. Place it near your plant in direct sunlight.
+ Using the tweezers and scissors, cut each blossom close to the base. Place them flat and facing upward. Cover the water in the bowl with one layer of flowers.
+ When you are finished, give thanks to the plant and state your intention for this essence.

Completing the Essence:

Allow the essence to remain in the sunlight for 3-4 hours. If this is a moon essence, then you can choose a full moon night and leave it under the full moon all night.

When the essence is done infusing, pour the water through the strainer into the jar and mix it with 50:50 solution of the alcohol or vinegar. Place the lid on the jar and label it with the flower name, date, and any magical symbols appropriate for this elixir.

This is called the Mother Essence. To make a stock essence, add 10 drops of the mother essence to a 60 ml. bottle and fill it with 50:50 spring water and alcohol or vinegar. To make a dosage bottle, add one drop of the essence from the stock bottle to a 15 ml. bottle filled with 50:50 spring water and alcohol or vinegar.

Usage:

+ **Internally:** To use, take 4-7 drops of your dosage essence, three times per day under the tongue or in water.
+ **Aura:** Add 15-30 drops of the dosage essence to a spray bottle and add water, then spray your aura as needed.

I used some guidance from this site combined with my own experience over the years. *

*Source: http://clinicalherbalism.com how-to-make-your-own-flower-essence/

Protection

This is a concept that in the very name implies that you need to protect yourself from something that can hurt you. Ultimately, there is nothing to fear. You are truly always held in Divine love if you focus on this.

But when we begin to work in the more esoteric realms and choose to work with energy in a conscious way, then we—in that very choice—open ourselves up to all kinds of understanding.

This is why, if you are going to do the Great Work of alchemical transformation, then first, you must be committed to managing your energy field.

You must be committed to caretaking your energy. What you put in your body will affect what you experience. Who you decide to share time and space with will affect your energy. How you spend your time will affect your energy. What you do with your energy and body will affect your life.

An Important Note About Alcohol and Drugs

Emotion/mind-altering substances have the quality of being a pathway for energies to enter a person's energetic field, mind, and body.

Alcohol is a substance that takes on vibrations very easily. That is why it is used to extract healing properties of herbs, as in making herbal tinctures, and is used in rituals for the purpose of taking in a certain intentional vibration. For example, wine has been used in ritual because it can be alchemized and charged with frequency very easily.

Because of this, I recommend you either abstain or bless and change the vibration of any alcohol that you ingest.

When you ingest alcohol without this intentionality, you open yourself up to any energies that want to come in. And, since alcohol takes on vibrations easily, that means anything within about a six-foot radius of it can be affected. So, when you order a drink in a bar, that alcohol has in it the energy of the person who poured it, the energy of the person who brought it to you, and the energy of the people at your table.

Think about that.

Once you ingest it, you also open up channels within yourself. If you are not conscious about this and taking intentional steps, you will be opening yourself to any energies that want to come in and feel or feed off your energy.

Similarly, with drugs—any kind, even marijuana and "plant medicine" like mushrooms and other psychedelics—they open up channels. If you are not in clear intention and do not create a Sacred Space, this opens up the possibility for any kind of energy to come in and attach to you.

When these things are used without sacred intention or in sacred ceremonial space, the person who is being affected by them will be vulnerable to all sorts of energies. And with hallucinogens, whatever chakras are blocked and at whatever level their kundalini energy is at is where they will experience their "high/journey." Without proper support, a person can get stuck at that level until they are cleared.

Hallucinations—or any chemically altered state of being—do not automatically create spiritual understanding.

The questions to ask yourself to discern whether your experience is supporting spiritual awakening or simply a chemical response are:

+ Did your experience give you universal gain?
+ Has your ego receded into the background, allowing your Higher Self to take on a more prominent role in guiding your life?
+ Do you feel like you have a connection to Source that is guiding you in more Unity?
+ Did you find inner peace and serenity?

- Are some of the habits, behaviors, thought patterns, or prejudices that you had beforehand dissolved?
- Are you navigating your life from a place of empowerment?
- Did your abuses or addictions dissolve?
- Are you a clearer vessel?

These are the things that you look for if it's a true spiritual experience. Everything else is just party games or the next trendy activity—and these can lead to people getting themselves even more clouded and disconnected from Source.

People think that using plant medicine is the old way, so it must be good. But this is not the full picture. Humans began to use plant medicine to gain access to the spiritual realm *as a result of already being disconnected from Source access.*

To experience your Divine connection, you require nothing external to yourself. This is the fundamental truth, the ancient reality. You were once perfectly connected, and the current belief that you are not is, in fact, a false notion.

You can access all the realms without any substances if you are willing to take your power back, be intentional about managing your energy, do the work necessary to keep transforming your inner landscape, and maintain a spiritual practice.

Basic Ways to Protect Yourself

Flowers

This is an easy way to have etheric flowers around you to help transmute energies that are less than Divine light and love before they can penetrate your auric field.

It is common to visualize roses for this, as they carry a very high, pure frequency. You can choose which color you would like, but imagine placing beautiful fresh rose blooms just outside your field in this order: front, left, right, back, above, and the earth below protects you.

These stay in place until you remove them. But as your day goes on, they will wither and fade as they do the job of absorbing any negative energy. So, during the course of your day, imagine checking them and replacing them. You can do this however often you would like, but it is best done, at least, at the change of tides. This means the flowers you put in place after sunrise will only hold until sunset. And likewise if you put them in place after sunset, they will only hold until sunrise.

To refresh your flowers, you imagine them and blow them up as if to see them disappear in the opposite order you placed them: start above, then behind you, right, left, and in front. Then go ahead and replace them in the order they were originally.

Earth & Heaven Circuit

Visualize an infinity symbol (the figure eight), preferably in a gold color, running from the Earth Star chakra below your feet up to touch the Soul Star chakra just above your head. Envision this running through your body and hold this current for 30 seconds or more.

Other Visualizations

+ Visualize yourself surrounded by a "bubble" of white light.
+ Visualize a Violet Flame radiating from your heart outward, creating a bubble of protection from the center of your heart chakra.

Any of these can be combined. Practice each one and feel them. That is what matters most—feel yourself experiencing a shift. That is how you know it is working. And layer these until you find the right combination that makes you feel expansive, clear, and powerful!

- 8th Soul Star Chakra
- 7th Crown Chakra
- 6th Third Eye Chakra
- 5th Throat Chakra
- 4th Heart Chakra
- 3rd Solar Plexus Chakra
- 2nd Sacral Chakra
- 1st Root Chakra
- 0 Earth Star Chakra

The Chakra System: Basics

Chakras are the energy centers of your body. The word "chakra" means "wheel" in Sanskrit and refers to the points of energy that spin along the center of your body, running along your spine. Keeping your chakras clear improves your life, allowing energy to flow freely. When these centers are open and aligned, your emotional, physical, mental, and spiritual health are balanced.

Earth Star Chakra

This is a few inches below your feet, is rooted in the Earth, and also touches your aura. It is the energy of sustenance that feeds your energy body.

1st Chakra—Base or Root Chakra (red)

This is the foundational chakra, connecting you to the Earth and this life. When balanced, you feel centered, supported, safe, and secure.

2nd Chakra—Sacral Chakra (orange)

This chakra governs sensuality, creativity, pleasure, and sexuality. When balanced, you have strong, nurturing relationships and enjoy life without excess, addictions, inhibitions, etc. You radiate harmony.

3rd Chakra—Solar Plexus (yellow)

Often known as the "personal power" chakra, it is associated with your self-confidence, self-esteem, and personal will. When balanced, you are motivated, confident, and empowered. You can manifest your intentions easily.

4th Chakra—Heart Chakra (green)

This chakra holds love for self and others, empathy, compassion, gratitude, and forgiveness. When balanced, you feel inner peace, unconditional love, joy, connection, appreciation for beauty, and in harmony with all.

5th Chakra—Throat Chakra (turquoise)

This chakra is the home of communication and self-expression. When balanced, you speak your truth confidently and clearly with love and compassion and feel a sense of being heard.

6th Chakra—3rd Eye Chakra (indigo)

This is where your intuition and imagination reside. When balanced, your psychic abilities are stronger, and you see life with more clarity and understand hidden truths.

7th Chakra—Crown Chakra (white/violet)

This chakra surrounds the crown of your head and is the center for spiritual enlightenment, connecting you to the universal consciousness. When balanced, you feel deeply connected, purposeful, serene, and at one with all that is.

Soul Star Chakra

This chakra is where your soul resides and is connected to your body. You can pull it down into the lower chakras when needed for healing. It is a bridge for our soul between the body and the higher realms.

How to Clear and Balance Chakras

You can use the previously described aura cleansing tools to clear your chakras, as well as sound from tuning forks and singing bowls, your hands, or your voice. Here are the corresponding Bija mantras ("Bija" means "seed" in Sanskrit) to chant aloud or silently to balance the five energy centers and the five elements associated with them:

Root.................. "LAM" .... Earth
Sacral .... "VAM" .... Water
Solar Plexus..... "RAM" .... Fire
Heart .... "YAM" .... Air
Throat.............. "HAM" .... Spirit/Ether
3rd Eye............. "SHAM" .... Spirit/Ether
Crown............. "OM"................. Spirit/Ether

Recap

The purification stage is all about cleansing and refining, transforming, and transmuting. These practices support purifying your body, mind, and spirit. With these tools, you are able to become a clearer vessel so your light and inner guidance can reside in you more fully. You will be able to sense more clearly and, as a result, your intuition and knowing become stronger. Your vessel is preparing to realign so your Divine connection can be fully restored and your personal empowerment returned.

Go Deeper

Reflect on the following to support this stage of transformation:

Health/Body

- What habits need to be released so that new, healthier ones can become your natural state?
- Which parts of your health or body need strengthening because they are depleted?
- Which parts of your health or body are telling you they need nourishment?
- Which parts of your health or body need to be cleansed or cleared out so that new growth can happen?
- What cleansing rituals will you do to cleanse and renew your body?

Love/Partnership/Relationships

+ What do you need to acknowledge about your self-love in order to heal?
+ What trauma are you still carrying around your body or sexuality?
+ What losses do you need to heal?
+ Who do you need to forgive?
+ Which relationships need nurturing?
+ Which relationships need to be let go?
+ What does partnership look like to you in its purest form?

There are places deep inside that we hide so that we can make peace and avoid showing our weakness. There are things we do to please others and things we have done because they are best for us but have still caused others pain.

All these things need to be reconciled.

Now is the time to become very honest with yourself and complete and heal these things. Are you carrying any pain within you from your family or lineage regarding these questions? It is time to let go of them now.

Explore these questions, let your emotions come to the surface, and use these clearing and purification techniques to transmute them, allowing them to rise to a higher frequency.

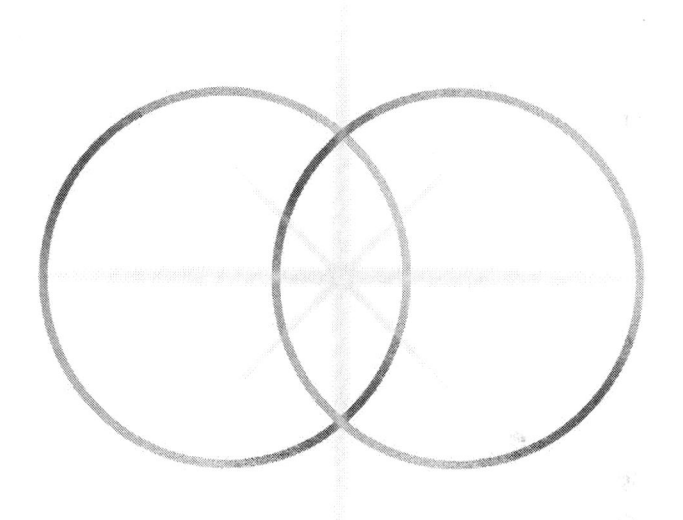

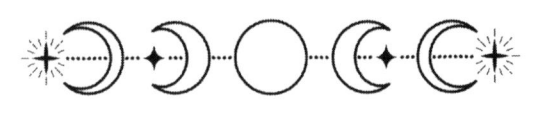

Garden

"Love Thyself" is all I can hear,
Then why does my heart break when you are not near?

I accept that your presence could one day disappear,
For now, that is something my Soul doesn't want to hear.

A life without you feels empty and serene,
A contradiction in my heart and mind. What does it mean?

To take from me the one constant that I had,
To give me my freedom, which could drive me mad.

Why do I remain tortured in this life I have made?
Trusting what you said, trusting what you gave.

Now in the garden of my Soul's creation,
Which path do I take to my heart's salvation?

—Sarah Michelle Wergin

Part 3: Rebirth

Now that you have dissolved the old life or ways of being and purified what remains, rebirth is the next stage of your transformation. And it can be happening as you are still purifying your life.

The process of rebirth can be quick or long, depending on the Soul. This process can take months or years. There is no right amount of time. And, of course, as with all the alchemical stages, one stage can be happening within other stages.

For example, during your Rebirth stage, you could be feeling great and alive and excited, and then—BAM! You get hit with something that brings you back into the Dissolution phase for a bit because there is another aspect to see, feel, and heal.

It doesn't mean something you did is not working. It doesn't mean you are being punished. It doesn't mean your life is never going to change. It doesn't mean any of these negative judgments your mind (or ego) would like to put on it. All it means is there is another layer that is coming up to be seen, acknowledged, and processed. So you go back into that with awareness and surrender and transmute that next layer.

This is how to navigate times of crisis: Remember that this is just another level of clearing and refining. You have your awareness. You allow whatever is happening to show you what emotion, thought, or behavior wants to come forth for transmutation. You reach for one of your "tools" and do the work.

It is normal along the journey of ascension, enlightenment, or evolution for this to happen. In fact, it never stops. There are just small layers and bigger layers. But shedding is always happening—just like our skin. We are constantly shedding old cells and birthing new, fresh ones.

We are always shedding old energies and opening to or creating new ones.

With Rebirth, you are fueled by the aliveness that came into you from Purification. You are like a newborn baby, full of hope and innocence for all the possibilities that lay before you. The passion fills you! You feel connected! A new zest for life and new ideas are flowing.

This can be a very ecstatic time. The elixir of creation is overflowing, and there is movement while, at the same time, a stillness of peace.

Remember at this stage to not collapse yourself into overjoy or allow the ego to take control again. Stay centered, grounded, and humble. A slow, smoldering fire creates more peace, enduring heat, and a more calculated outcome than a blaze out of control that burns bright and then dies out.

This is the perfect time to cultivate new healthy habits and learn new techniques that create more energy and livelihood for yourself in the long run.

This requires you to really take stock of your true priorities for your life and then put systems in place that will support giving yourself those things. You are not meant to do everything yourself. Thinking outside the box with your renewed energy and insight can allow you to see how you can delegate things to other people that will support them to thrive, as they help you do what you are meant to do.

Our evolution and expansion are meant to fill our chalice so that it is overflowing and we can give to others. Our process will bring results, not just for ourselves but for so many people around us, as well.

As you are becoming more your new self, give yourself permission to reflect. Give yourself much praise and love for all the work and dedication you offered and for the trials you went through. Give yourself so much love and recognition for your accomplishment of being where you are now.

Too many do not take the time to do this. They come out of the difficult parts and feel the inertia of the rebirth, and then are off and running again.

But in order for you to cultivate more and more self-love (not false ego love, but true love of self), you must take the time to sit, look into the eyes of your inner child, and speak the words of praise and acknowledgment so your inner child feels seen, recognized, and appreciated.

These are the things so many of us were lacking as children.

This lack creates the cycle of unmet needs, which becomes the wounding. Then you end up in adulthood seeking all of that from the outside and setting yourself up for all of your relationships to be a reflection of every wound you still have not healed. You carry that from one relationship to the next until you learn that you actually have to give that to yourself. Once it is inside you, you will attract it from your partner.

So much discontent and suffering can be cleared by this realization.

And the way to do this is by taking the time—because you are worth it!—to slow down, look at all your hard work, your dedication, your accomplishments, and give yourself praise and love. Treat yourself to some downtime, to something that acknowledges your efforts, and hold yourself in that light and love before you go full speed ahead into the new.

The more you do this, the more whole you will become.

During this time, you're reinventing who you are going to be moving forward. All you have to do each day when you wake up is ask yourself, "What is my highest path of light and joy today?" Then do that. You will be on the right path if you do.

Tools: Manifestation

Now that you are reborn, it's time to manifest your wildest dreams for this lifetime. How do you do that? You follow this (not always so simple) recipe:

The first ingredient is FREE WILL

It's essential that you genuinely desire to do this; it can't be driven by someone else's wishes. This journey requires wholehearted commitment and cannot be compelled. If you're not fully invested, feeling pressured, or approaching it half-heartedly, believing you can deceive your Soul or Higher Self, or if you're hoping to simply close your eyes and have someone else do the work, then your outcomes will likely be underwhelming, or they may even fail entirely.

The second ingredient is DEDICATION

You must follow through all the way and not stop part of the way through. Dedication means you are giving it your best effort and you are making a commitment to see it through, even when it is not easy or fun. The dedication is to yourself. You are saying, "I AM worth it!"

The third ingredient is a sprinkle of your ESSENCE

This is an interesting ingredient because you don't have to use all of your essence. Essence is infinite, and just a sprinkle of it actually replicates infinitely. This means that you don't have to know at this stage the entirety of who and what you are. Many people have concepts, but, in reality, most people have not merged with them entirely. So, you give a sprinkle, some little bit of what you know you are. For example, you feel you are pretty good at making things sound exciting so you can get others (like your kids) to want to do an activity. Well, do that for yourself! Get creative and set up what you need to get excited about this journey.

The fourth ingredient is a handful of INTENTION

This is the activating ingredient! The one that makes the brew begin to boil. This will be the passion that is rising for yourself and your life at this moment. This can come into awareness from the Self or from your spiritual guides or guardians. What is it you want to create or experience now? This is the ingredient that is your "vision," a glimpse of what your life can be. Use this as motivation!

The fifth ingredient is OPENNESS

Become open like a chalice or like a lid opening. This allows for the movement to begin, like boiling the separate ingredients into something new. Openness is allowing space for all the things you have not or are not able to see that could happen or come your way. Openness is what makes it possible to receive something new. Resistance will only keep pushing things away.

The sixth ingredient is SURRENDER

Release it! It has been put into motion. The inertia is at work, and the result will be what it will be. Allow for the magic to happen when all the Divine forces collectively come together to bring something into form or reality that you didn't expect or imagine. Don't try to push the river or pull up the flower before its time. Trust and allow.

The last ingredient is GRATITUDE

Give thanks for all the help and all the blessings that are here and coming. The brew is done. You are now in a completely changed internal environment than when you started. A whole new frequency is within you. Just keep giving thanks and allow the feeling to come deeply into your body, mind, and Soul. Let it seep in…little by little…and acknowledge each sensation of this and each blessing that does come your way. See them, acknowledge them, and give thanks. Say, "More, please!" This is how you tell the Universe, "YES! Keep it coming!"

Phases of the Moon

Manifestation is also influenced by the phases of the Moon. Being mindful and tapping into the energies of at least the New Moons and Full Moons can provide important support for bringing what you desire into your life. Each phase lasts approximately six to eight days within the 29-day cycle. There are numerous mobile apps and websites that you can tap to track its movement. Generally, it takes one Moon cycle to see any effects.

New Moon

This phase has to do with the seed or inception of things. Setting intentions for what you would like to see grow, manifest, or come to fruition in the coming cycles.

Waxing Crescent

This phase supports all types of positive or increasing intentions and new beginnings. This is the increasing light and energy phase of the Moon cycle. Think of things growing. Invoking inspiration, energy, creativity, vitality, and expansion in any area.

First Quarter

This is the phase for attracting things to you as the energy continues to grow in power: business, prosperity, friendships, luck, setting new goals, and wishes.

Waxing Gibbous

This phase is about the development and strengthening of things already in existence or underway. You are tending to your seeds that have sprouted, so work with patience, peace, and harmony as you caretake them.

Full Moon

Full Moon intentions can be harnessed three days prior and three days after. This is the most powerful time for working with areas needing protection, for using the skill of divination, honoring spirits, or calling to ancestors. This period is all about things coming to completion, fruition, and also release. And you are seeing if your seeds are bearing fruit. What needs to be harvested and what is now time to let go of? It is a time to ask for things and give thanks when they are done!

Waning Gibbous

This is a phase of rejecting negative things in our lives, including illness and disease, and letting go of things. Releasing anything less than love. This is the phase to do banishing rituals.

Last Quarter

This is a phase that continues to carry the force for things coming to an end, banishing energies you no longer want, releasing addictions or habits. It is all about letting go.

Waning Crescent

This is the phase for intentions to do with change, removing obstacles, separation from things, or can be used to help draw love or money or something else to you by removing sorrows and past hurts. It carries a calming, protective, serene energy. But remember, three days before the New Moon is called the Dark Phase of the Moon, and it is best to be still, reflect, and do no magic.

Exercise: New Moon Intentions

The New Moon represents new beginnings. It is the time to sow seeds, to take your unmanifested intentions, desires, visions, and creations, and hold them in your hand.

Literally! HOLD OUT YOUR HANDS! See them there. How many appear to you right now?

Look down and see how many there are. Hold them in your hand and look at them all.

Just like with all seeds in the natural world, there will be some that don't need to be planted right now and some that will not take root. There will be some that are outdated or old, and you need to discard them because they might be related to an old version of yourself.

Feel the vision of each seed, and let the details reveal themselves to you. What they would feel like in this moment, what the future might look like with them. Take yourself into that vibration.

From there, you will feel if there is any distortion or discord.

So, let's say a seed has an old energy in it. When you feel into it, and you envision it—even though it might have been something that you wanted before (and maybe even still think you want)—really let yourself feel it from a new point of YOU! Not a new "point of view," a new YOU!

Without any attachment to it, how does it feel?

If there is a heaviness, a sense of burden, a sense of hardness, or if your energy contracts in any way, this is not the path of highest light for you. An idea could require a lot of effort or work, but you would feel excited about that effort or work, not heavy or burdened if it's a good path for you.

Sit with it and see if it's just a detail about the seed that needs to be changed, or if it's the whole seed that needs to be discarded.

Now look at the ones that might show up to you as things you still want, but maybe it's not the right time to plant the seed or move forward with it. Allow your energy to harmonize with the frequency of that. Really feel into it.

If we try and push things before it's their time, all we get is resistance, frustration, and disappointment, which can lead to doubting our own guidance, intuition, and self, when in reality, it's just not the right time!

Now look at the seeds that are left. Are they bright? Do they shine? Do they radiate? Do they feel good? Can you feel them in your body, making you feel more alive? That's what you're looking for! The seed should make you feel more alive!

If the idea makes you feel exhausted, then it is either not the right time, some aspect of it needs to change, or the whole idea needs to be discarded because it is not right for you.

Your seeds of intentions should light you up! They should feel exciting, happy, expanding, and vibrant. Now, look at each one. What are they related to? See the details and see the nuances.

Now ask yourself—your Higher Self: Is it time to put it into place now with this New Moon?

If the answer is yes, then write down the details that you feel, sense, and know. Take these into your ceremony. Allow yourself to envision or allow the vision to come to you, then feel the frequency of how they would feel, how your life would feel. Run it through you. And hold this for as long as you can. It could be 17 seconds, it could be a minute, it could be five minutes.

As soon as you're not able to hold it anymore, then let it go and finish your ceremony in whatever way you choose, as you offer it up to the Divine for support.

Sample New Moon Ritual

1. Gather supplies.
2. Open Sacred Space.
3. Light a candle.
4. Add water into the chalice.
5. Salt refreshed.
6. Incense burning.
7. Breathing, clearing, getting centered.
8. Write your intentions, wishes, and seeds with a particular pen color and type of paper.
9. Draw symbols with essential oil.
10. Folding paper three times—away from you if it is something you want to release, or toward you if you want to bring it to you.
11. Burn the paper.
12. Give thanks.
13. Close circle/Sacred Space.

After you've done all of that, what is the next step?

This is the most crucial step that most people forget or bypass. After you've done all of the visualization, all of the action, and even the gratitude afterward, now what do you do?

You must surrender.

You have to let it go completely. Otherwise, it cannot come back to you. If you are still holding onto it…and checking it…and checking it…and checking it…you're still holding onto it.

It has to be released from your field and go into the Universe to have the Divine work its magic.

Divine makeup. Divine alignment. Divine support. Divine timing. All of those pieces have to come together for the highest and best version of this to come to you.

The "Divine makeup" is the design, how it will actually look with the details. Usually, it's going to look a little different than you thought. The "Divine alignment" is the synergy it has with the other ripples that it is meeting and will affect. The "Divine support" is all of the people and their lives that have to come together to support this and it coming to you. "Divine timing" is the precise moment when everything and all aspects have aligned, and the current is open for it to make its way to you.

So, after your ceremony, surrender! Let it go completely. Trust and allow the Divine to do its thing for you and the greater whole. Give it time. Just keep giving thanks as if it's already done. "I am so grateful (insert desire/want/need) is done." "I am so grateful (insert desire/want/need) in my life." Or use an "I have____in my life" statement. And stay with that. Then, the seeds have what they need to sprout.

And if they do not sprout, remember this: it is the ESSENCE of what you want that will make its way to you. That could show up in a way you never thought about.

Exercise: Full Moon Intentions

The Full Moon represents completion, things coming to fruition or releasing. It is the time to state what you are complete with and want to be done with, what you want to see come to its full potential, or what you want to release.

It can be a time to see the seeds that you have sown become realized. Your intentions, desires, visions, and creations—giving thanks for their completion, manifestation, or what needs to be released as to make room for a different creation or outcome. It is also a great time to cut cords, clear attachments, and sever bonds.

Look at what you have created, and give thanks for the completion. Visualize it coming to fruition and what that will look like if it isn't done yet. Also, take stock of what no longer may be good for you and release it at this time. See a new path or outcome.

Let the things you have created go. Give thanks.

Feel into what you need to release to make room for the new to come in the next cycle. If you are releasing, see any strings, cords, or attachments being cut and falling away. See yourself feeling freer and freer as you visualize any lines between you and someone else (or something else) being released. Know that it creates a freedom for yourself and also for them, and for you to be restored to your full power. No more being drained, but also no more "pulling" on someone else either. You will experience a coming back to yourself. This is a gift for each person.

Feel in your body as the details reveal themselves to you. What would they feel like in this moment? What might the future look like with them? Take yourself into that vibration.

From there, you will feel if there is any distortion or discord.

This is a perfect time to assist yourself, get out of your own way, and step aside as you allow for the power of the pull of the Moon to start the magic to deliver to you what you want to see come into being.

Set the intention to magnetize to you with ease and grace.

Without any attachment to the outcome, just the gratitude. Knowing that what you asked for may end up showing up in your life experience in an infinite amount of ways. Stay open.

Sample Full Moon Ritual

1. Gather supplies.
2. Open Sacred Space.
3. Light a candle.
4. Add water into the chalice.
5. Salt refreshed.
6. Incense burning.
7. Breathing, clearing, getting centered.
8. Write your gratitude, what you want to see in its fullest, or what you want to release.
9. Draw symbols with essential oil.
10. Fold paper three times—away from you if it is something you want to release, or toward you if you want to bring it to you.
11. Burn the paper.
12. Give thanks.
13. Close circle/Sacred Space.

Astrology

You are born with a blueprint of what your Soul came here for. There are parts that are certain and parts that are vague enough to allow space for the free will to create. Astrology is one way to understand more about yourself so that you can use your free will in a more positive and harmonious way.

Most people know their Sun Sign, but that is such a small part of the overall picture! Gaining some understanding of your chart can help you use your gifts with more wisdom. Astrology can cause confusion or clarity, depending on who is giving you the guidance. Use discernment when choosing a person to read your charts.

The three big pieces are the Sun Sign, which is your overall personality, but the Rising/Ascendant Sign is really how you act in the world and how people see you. Your Moon Sign is how you are emotionally. Another big piece is your North Node. This represents the unfinished business from another lifetime that you are bringing into this life to work on.

Starting with just these few aspects of your chart can help you better understand yourself, your life, and others.

Numerology

"Everything in Heaven and on Earth is arranged according to numerological discipline."

—Linda Goodman, author of *Star Signs*

This ancient practice is a basic understanding of the makeup of the Universe.

There are many systems of numerical alphabets and numerological systems. Many people have written on this topic, and there are so many sources that state what they believe the meanings assigned to each number are.

But in truth, there is only one numerical alphabet that is real, and only one system of calculating these numbers that is reliable and true. These are the

Chaldean and Kabbalah systems handed down by the ancient Chaldeans and the Hebrew Kabbalah.

This system—when used properly—will give you great insight into your energy. You can do these calculations on your name, your birthdate, your address, etc. Anything with letters or numbers can be calculated to find out what the energy of that "thing" is radiating.

This can help you understand what experiences you may deal with in your life.

With this knowledge, you can take a more co-creative approach and work with the spelling of names to change the energy you radiate into the world. You can also use this tool to check on the vibration of a place you live by doing the calculations on the address.

Granted, it is only one piece of the puzzle that will be influencing your experience. Our astrology plays a role. The Feng Shui of the dwelling we live and work in plays a role. The thoughts we have play a role. The foods we put in our bodies play a role. All of these things make up how we will experience our life.

It is helpful when you are beginning to shape what kind of energy you wish to be in the world that you take stock of all these influences.

You may decide to change the way you spell your name or maybe choose a whole new name. You may choose between two different apartments because one has a better numerological meaning for you. You could soften the intensity of your birth number by the name you go by in the world. The list goes on.

Recap

The Rebirth stage is about rebuilding or renewing yourself. It is a living resurrection. The new YOU! New life. New beginnings. These tools give you a few universal keys to assist you in creating your new self. This ancient knowledge will open doors for you to explore the great mysteries even deeper and offer you systems to support you going forward.

Go Deeper

Pause and reflect on these questions to help you with this stage:

Play/Fun/Joy

+ What joy have you lost? What are things that you do for fun? Where in your life do you make playtime?
+ There was a time when play was all you knew because nothing was asked of you yet, so you were discovering this incredible, fun new world.
+ When did you lose that wonder?
+ Now that you are reclaiming your true self, what things do you enjoy that are purely for fun?
+ Where in your life can you make playtime each day?
+ How can all the things you do each day be done joyfully?

Prosperity/Abundance

Abundance is more than money. It can be expressed in any aspect of life: money, good health, free time, work you love, etc. Think of it as the benevolent fullness that overflows: you have all you need and more, so you can give.

+ What blocks do you have around the concept of abundance?
+ Up until now, how did you define abundance?
+ Make a list of all the areas of your life that are lacking abundance.
+ What areas of your life are abundant?
+ What steps do you need to take to make room for abundance to come in for all that you need and want?
+ What are you willing to give up to receive abundance? One of the keys to abundance is that you must let go of something else to make room for it to come in…that could be as simple as doubt!

Children/Your Creations in the World

+ What issues need to be healed with your children?
+ What needs do they have that pull on you?
+ What ties are time to release?
+ What relationship dynamics need to be transformed around the topic of children?
+ Is your creativity blocked in any way?
+ What new creations are in your heart's desire?
+ Where are you delaying your creation?

All these questions are to be asked of yourself related to actual children (which can be a person/people or animal you nurture), as well as all creative projects that you have created or are being guided to create. This is about CREATION in all forms. It is also about looking at where, what, and who you nurture. What is not in alignment with your new vibration? How can you transform it?

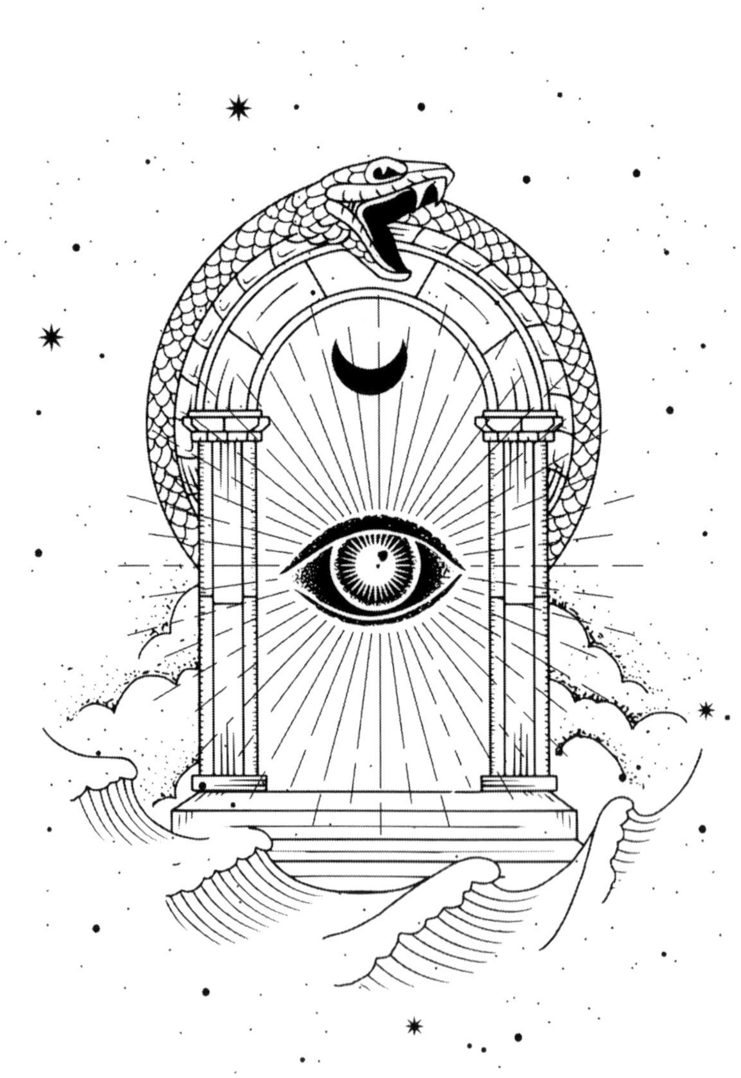

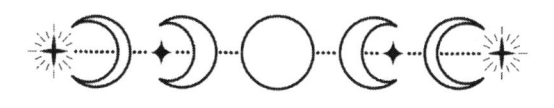

Doorway

Limitless wonder I call upon you,
Know your daughter as pure and true.

Ask not why I steal from you,
I take only what was given, and you always knew.

Open the doorway so I may step through.

Touch my heart so I may see,
Sing to my ears so I may know,
Expand my awareness in the eternal glow.

All that I am,
The Divine does give.
But I must take my leave,
so my Soul can Live.

Separate to remember,
Veil to discover,
Forget to uncover,
Expose the pretender.

I will return one day,
When all is complete,
Through the Doorway of the house,
That I left to Seek.

—Sarah Michelle Wergin

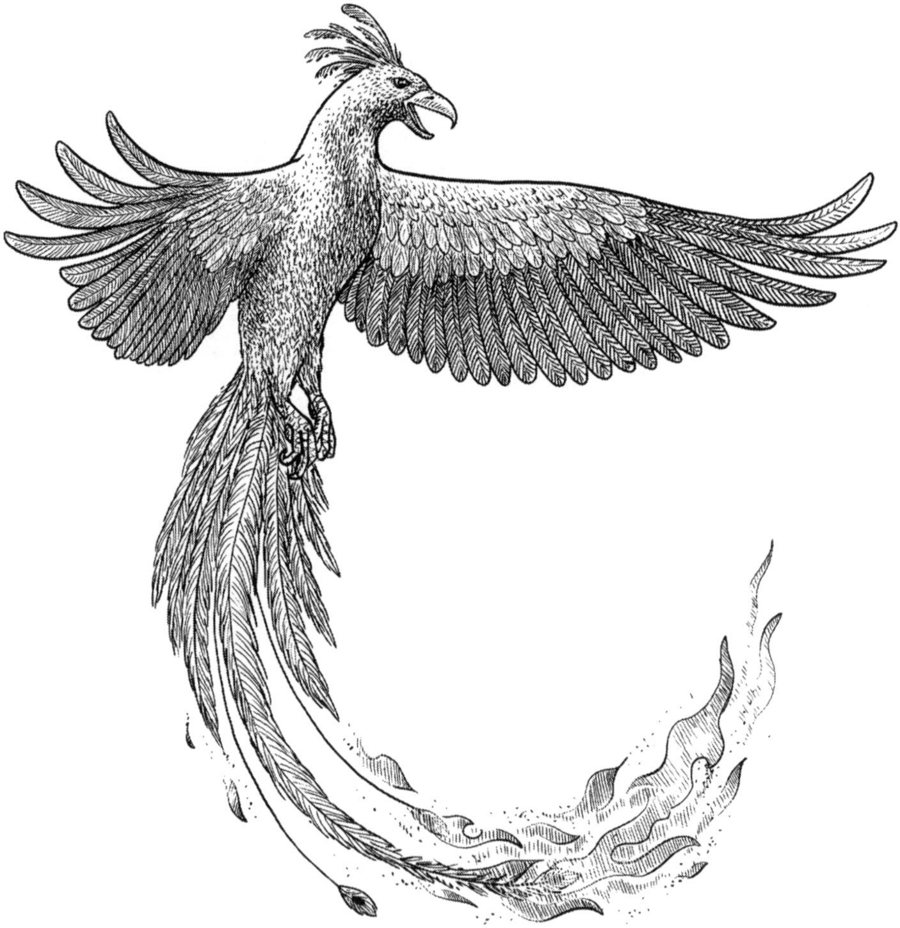

Living in Divine Union

It is time for a recalibration into a truly new way of BEING on Earth. There is potential for a completely new adventure. CHOOSING to step onto that path is the beginning.

When you are finally tired of repeating your past experiences, behaviors, ancestral patterns, and planetary patterns, it's time to wake up to your evolved self—the Divine Union.

Break your old patterns, thoughts, emotional expressions, and behaviors. Release all that is within you to be transformed. Surrender and allow it all to transmute. This is how you can meet your true self.

You have agreements with other Souls to come here and play a role with them. It serves to teach you your lessons. As you grow and evolve, you can change the "role" you have been playing for anything, anyone, or any place. You will know when it is time to begin anew.

Embodying your new essence will lead the way to you playing an enlightened role for yourself and others. It may not be what it seems. Look for the truth between the words, and you will know. Be brave enough to listen to the quiet inner voice, even when it seems like stepping into the unknown.

You are much more than your current role has been portraying.

You have chosen the play, but once you are tired enough of the current drama, you will cry out for the TRUTH. The truth will present you with a new stage, and the new stage isn't outside of yourself, as you have thought.

"Something needs to change in my life! My job…my family…my relationship…my country!"

You will never retire from that drama if you still see it as something outside yourself.

When you are so tired that you sit still and close your eyes, you will turn inside, even for a moment. And in that moment, you will be transported into the realm of all your possibilities.

Living Truth

It's important for us to uncover the layers of who we truly are. As we do our inner work on our path of evolution and transformation, we are constantly peeling back layers.

Even when you are aligned, even when you are awake, you are still in your process.

As you progress towards enlightenment, your awareness expands, turning you into a keen observer of your experiences. But you still need to adjust, you still need to stay vigilant, and, for those on the path of mastery, it is the Great Work.

It takes dedication and devotion to stay on this path.

You will be tested, but that is what you signed up for. It is why you incarnated—to grow. A Soul cannot grow and evolve without being tested. And the tests are not some sort of trap set up by "God" for you to have to go through and then judge you as "He" watches you suffer.

The truth is, the tests were set up by you. They were *agreements.*

Your Higher Self was at the table of Creation, looking down at a map. This map is your Soul's path (or story), for it can be told in pictures or words, but it is just an energetic blueprint. It is looking down at the map that shows its origination of differentiation all the way through to its reintegration into its origination. From Source back to Source.

With its mission in mind, it contemplates the potential routes, possible stops, detours and their destinations, the challenges along each path, the hazards inherent to specific routes, the mountains to overcome, the rivers to cross for passage to the other side, the potential encounters with new people, the resting places for the night, the oceans to navigate, and foreign lands that might create feelings of loneliness or uncertainty.

And so much else that is possible.

Surveying the entire map, you formulated your plan and devised a mutually agreed-upon strategy. Deliberately, you selected the two individuals you wished to incarnate with and determined the starting point of your journey. You made choices regarding the environment for your upbringing and the culture that would shape you. All this, with the awareness that upon entering that life or shoreline, your mission would commence. Endowed with free will, you could utilize your navigation system (intuition from your Higher Self/Soul) at any point along the way to guide and assist you in making choices.

Certain destinies, events, and individuals are predetermined in your journey. Yet, the variables arise from each individual Soul within the collective exercising their free will, making unpredictable choices that ripple through the fabric of your experience. This results in the creation of various paths that may open or close. Some roads or doors are predestined, while others become possible only because of decisions made by you or someone else.

But it is all the journey, the mission that you set out to embark on so long ago.

It serves as the playground where you're granted the stage to undergo trials that both burn and purify your soul while also experiencing the ecstasy that fosters new expansion and possibilities.

And you did it all with love and devotion to God/dess, Self, Divinity, LIFE.

So, as the layers come off, your truths can change. Because sometimes the truths are attached to a particular layer of you, at a particular time, that now has been shed. There is a new awareness, there is a new light, there is a new understanding. So from that place, we allow for change, and we are allowed to understand new truths.

At the same time, you may hold steadfast core truths throughout your entire life. Some of these truths can serve as profound teachers, especially in instances where you are urged to understand your boundaries. When something doesn't feel right, it could be an indicator of a truth you already know and should listen to. Or, it might require further exploration to gain a deeper understanding of that truth.

The reason why it matters is that truth is what will sit hand-in-hand with your Soul.

When you betray your truth, you betray your Soul.

And then there's a wounding that happens. The betrayal of your Soul is our greatest wound. We can get wounded by others, seemingly outside ourselves, but we can also wound ourselves by abandoning ourselves, lying to ourselves, or abusing ourselves.

You see, these are the last frontiers for the awakening Soul.

The betrayal of ourselves is the starting point. This means that if you have come to the place where you stay true to yourself, then no matter what happens from the outside, you still have an open connection with your Higher Self that helps you not take on or take in too much of what someone else does. You have maintained a degree of your energy seal. That helps you to stay clear on what is a projection versus what is really yours.

If a person begins to betray themselves, these create weaknesses in the energy field, which can, over time, become holes for other energies (lower frequencies, ones that match the low frequency that caused the weakness) to pierce the aura and then attach to the body (mental, emotional, physical, spiritual, etc.).

If left unaddressed and unresolved, this pattern intensifies over time, triggering a spiral effect. Various distortions may manifest and play out in the individual's life, reinforcing the frequencies and beliefs that they carry. The external environment starts mirroring this distorted reality because it aligns with the energy the person is projecting. It becomes a reflection of that distortion.

Without proper support or intervention, this pattern can perpetuate cycles of repetition. If the individual does not find a way to break free from this cycle, it may persist throughout their entire life. If left unresolved, it could extend beyond the current lifetime, persisting and following the Soul into subsequent incarnations until it is finally cleared.

Distortions are created, and they can look like reality or truths, but really, they are false illusions.

And these distortions just sit there, waiting to someday be seen for what they truly are.

This is where truths fall away (as with the layers), dissolve, or become transmuted and integrated as a Soul heals and becomes clearer and clearer.

One prayer that assists this process of awakening is:

Call upon your chosen Divinity to VANQUISH ALL ILLUSION, ADVERSITY, SIN (remembering that this is just the word for something that "goes against goodness,") AND ARTIFICE OF EVIL.

And when we do this, we are asking (as with vanquishing) that all is absorbed back into the light, as if we are using our most powerful and pure energy of unconditional love. There is no dark or light in love. All duality vanishes at that point and just becomes love.

We are all going through this process of clearing distortions within ourselves on a massive scale. Some are doing this work more rapidly than others. And that is our offering.

As we do this work, we are not only doing it for ourselves but for every other Soul that carries that same pattern.

Those of us committed to the path of the Great Work have undertaken this mission as an act of love and support. Our endeavors extend beyond personal motivations. As we navigate through turmoil, suffering, or pain, we sit on a metaphorical throne, performing this work for the benefit of an entire kingdom.

Remember this when you feel alone or overwhelmed: it is not just you that you are helping.

Even if it appears to be only you in that space, any other Soul that has that same imprint is being served by the unwavering devotion that you have to vanquish that "demon" within yourself. And you watch it change around you.

We are all doing this together.

Prayer

Prayer is the way humans talk to the Divine. The way we pray makes a difference in the outcome of our experience and its effect on our life.

For a prayer to work in the way the Universe is designed, you need to state what you want as if it is already happening and true, then give thanks that it IS in your life. And then let it go.

When you beg and plead as "prayer" for what you want, the energy you are running through your body is the fear, sadness, or anger of the thing you want not being true right now.

This is old programming.

Organized religion teaches us that we need to be submissive and act like a groveling servant to get our prayers answered and our needs or wants met. The paradigm, set up to use fear and shame as ways to guilt people into submission, is a human-created system for those in power to keep the masses doing what they want.

Recognize this now. You are Divinely embodied and the co-creator in this play called Life.

You know about energy, power, and manifestation. Take your Divinely-given right to inner power and sovereignty back. Return to your original state, which is love and light.

From this place, you run the energy of being in alignment with our Divine Father/Mother that guides us and is in us. We are Unified or IN UNION.

Be in trust until the desire you have matches the image of the reality on the outside.

Hold the torch and keep the faith. Watch your thoughts, caretake your energy, and transform your emotions. Stay the course. Do the "work" and, in all things, remember love.

Then, when the thing, opportunity, or reality shows up, see it for what it is—perfectly manifested in Divine time for what you need. Realize that it is the essence in all things that matters, not the thing itself.

For example, say you want more money. What is the thing or feeling that the money will give you? That is what you are actually looking for: call THAT forth from the Universe and see all the ways in which it comes to you. It may look like money, yes, or it could look like support, new friends, or an unexpected opportunity.

What Living in Divine Union Looks Like

We all come here to Earth to play out different roles and experiences to fulfill us. One person's Living Union could look like being a monk and living in a cave, and another could be being a rock star and singing to masses of people

Putting esoteric ideas into practice and deciding to live a conscious life each day simply takes commitment and devotion.

The common factor for each person who is in Living Union is:

They are embodying their essence in a way that is in integrity throughout every layer of their BEING, from the human aspect of them, connected to their Soul, connected to their spirit, and connected to God/dess or Source.

A day of living in full embodiment might look like this:

Begin your day by waking up at your preferred time. Before stepping out of bed, express gratitude for your blessings and acknowledge the positive aspects you're looking forward to or currently experiencing in your life.

Start the day with devotional practices such as ceremony, meditation, prayer, or yoga, with a focus on mindful breathing. Engage in your spiritual rituals and journal any insights, ideas, or wisdom that arise.

Alternatively, indulge in quiet contemplation while sipping your morning hot beverage to nourish your body and spirit. Follow this with eating nourishing food to fuel your body.

During your bath or shower, incorporate skin brushing or chakra clearing to balance your body. Enhance the experience by adding essential oils to body oil or an aura spray, fostering a sense of self-love and care before venturing into the world.

Throughout the day, incorporate intentional movement, choosing activities that align with your energy and soul's needs. Whether it's a jog, Pilates, or gentle practices like Qi Gong or Tai Chi, prioritize movements that honor your well-being each day.

Engage in your soul work for the day by focusing on activities that bring you the highest joy. Even when faced with tasks that may seem unpleasant, boring, or frustrating, consider the end result and its impact on your sense of fulfillment and accomplishment. Change your mindset about less desirable tasks, infusing creativity to shift their energy and elevate their frequency. For example, if working on a computer, bring a beautiful flower, a picture of your favorite place, and a cup of tea to make the experience enjoyable.

Your daily work serves as an opportunity to assess if you are truly living in alignment with your aliveness. The tasks you undertake should uplift your energy; if you feel dread, tightness, heaviness, or a decrease in energy, it's a sign that something needs to change—either the entire path or the way you approach it creatively.

During meal times, choose nourishing food and drink intentionally, creating a peaceful setting with positive thoughts and conversation.

As the day concludes, spend time in front of your altar for ceremony or meditation, or connect with nature. Grounding with your feet on the earth, particularly at the day's end, helps discharge energy from computers and cell phones, allowing your body to recalibrate and exchange ions with Mother Earth for clearing and healing.

Express gratitude before sleep, acknowledging the blessings of the day. This fosters an energy of abundance and cultivates an attitude of gratitude, contributing to positive manifestations. Be mindful of your thoughts before bed, as they influence your subconscious. Giving thanks for the good things in your life is a positive practice. Ensure you prioritize an optimal bedtime to receive the proper amount of rest.

And what happens when a challenge or crisis strikes?

When your life throws a crisis at you, the first thing you must do is pause. Always.

Stop, take a breath, observe, and assess what should come next. It is always best to pause before you respond.

Then look at what is happening, who is involved, and the part you really need to play. Often, you may not need to do anything. But it is common for humans to feel a sense of self-importance and believe they have to play a role.

What if the best thing you could do is to wait, do nothing, or be silent?

Once you've assessed the situation's requirements, you select your spiritual tools. Drawing from the knowledge presented in this book or elsewhere, you choose the tools that will most effectively guide you through the crisis at hand.

Your commitment to spiritual practice enhances your clarity, granting you increased capability to navigate stress and crises compared to your previous state.

Even when confronted with intense pain, the extent and duration of suffering are influenced by your proactive choice and the application of your chosen tools. It's akin to the Samurai who centers himself with a breath before unsheathing his sword, the archer who takes deliberate aim, aligning her bow before releasing the arrow or to the Kung Fu master who, in a moment of danger, assesses the situation before applying the perfect amount of force.

Strategies for Living in Divine Union when presented with crisis or challenges:

+ Pause, take stock, do not suffer for suffering's sake.
+ Allow your feelings.
+ Observe them and integrate them.
+ Shift the focus off the emotion and back toward the solution.
+ Collect yourself back into center.
+ Decide which skills you will use.
+ Go into ceremony to get clarity and strategy.
+ Remember who you are, and call back all your power.
+ And then set yourself on your path from this aligned embodiment.
+ Go forth and conquer the challenge or crisis with the full force of your Divine Light and Love.

Recap

This phase marks the fruition of your inner journey, the culmination of the ongoing process you initiated. Like every stage, it signifies not an end but a continuous evolution. These practices serve to deepen your understanding of what it truly means to embody this path each day. With your Divine Union now restored, you assume the throne as the Sovereign of your own life. In complete connection, hand-in-hand with the Great One of ALL THAT IS, you live in alignment with your Soul and life mission.

Go Deeper

Here are some questions to help you process this stage and further your growth…

Life's Work/Career = Life Purpose

Life Purpose comes from what you are here to DO (where your life + Soul purpose intersect)

+ What did I love to do as a child?
+ What activity makes me the happiest?
+ What environment do I receive the most inspiration and joy from?
+ At the end of a day, if I have done ____, I feel complete.
+ What activities drain me? If I try and DO____, I always feel let down, depleted, unhappy.

Soul Imprint/Power/Gift = Soul Purpose/Mission

Soul Purpose comes from what you are here to BE.

+ When you were a child, what things or ideas did you inherently know?
+ When you have a great day, and you feel you are the best version of yourself, what does that look like? What things come naturally to you? List them.
+ If no one were to judge you, what would your perfect life look like?
+ First, write down what you THINK your gifts are. Then, write down what you KNOW your gifts are (do this fast—without thinking). What are the differences?

Family

Even if you lack a significant or any biological family, this principle still holds true in the context of your spiritual family: *"There is family and there is blood, sometimes they are not the same."* If all your family has passed, you still have them in your cells and memory. Also, any form of life (animals, plants, etc.) can be "family."

+ What issues need to be healed with any family members?
+ What needs do they have that pull on you?
+ Where do you need energy to support them?
+ What ties are time to release?

- What relationship dynamics need to be transformed?
- How can you take all family members out of the box of the past and allow them to be different? This will open the energy for them to do the same with you.
- What do you need to do in your life to feel abundance?
- What areas need to be filled up so they can overflow?
- What would it feel like to have all your needs and desires met when you have them?

Community/Earth

Above all, the Earth serves as our home and encompasses everything. Her creatures form our community, and without her and the diverse flora and fauna, our existence would cease. The human community we inhabit requires restoration; it ails, evident in symptoms such as violence, depression, and isolation. Despite a society heavily reliant on technology and modern conveniences to supposedly afford more time for personal pursuits, it has paradoxically fostered disconnection. We find ourselves more estranged from nature, other individuals, and even our own selves than ever before.

- Where in yourself do you feel anger towards your fellow human?
- How often do you sit outside under the stars and soak in the stillness?
- How often do you sit or lay on the earth?
- What needs do you ignore because you are too busy working at your job because it is how you "pay your bills?"
- How much time do you dedicate to nurturing love and joy with your family, friends, or neighbors? Reflect on the daily, weekly, or monthly tasks essential for caring for yourself and your family—tasks that, in a tribal society, might be shared responsibilities. Imagine the sense of support and collaboration that would bring. How would that feel?

These are questions to ask yourself. See your existence in a new way. Rediscover what it means to share, have help, and receive support when needed.

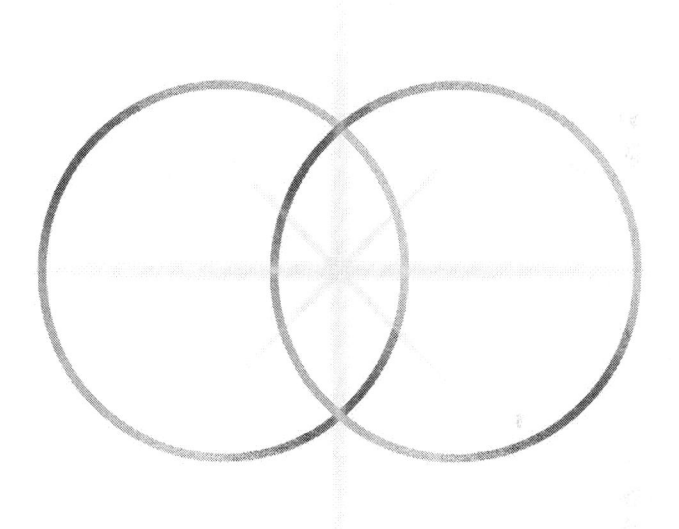

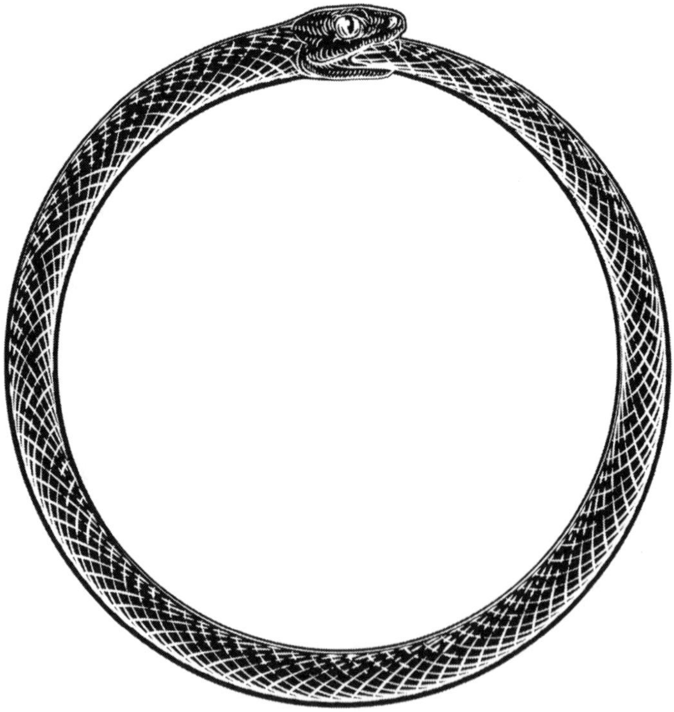

Conclusion

Each incarnation, whether on this planet or another, in this Universe or another, has a "purpose."

There is a PURPOSE to your incarnation, or you wouldn't be incarnating anymore.

The "experience of the lessons" is the reason. The purpose is evolution and then, the mission is what your Soul desires to be and do while in that incarnation—as a whole, as a part, as a role, as a witness, and as a participant.

Who or what did you come here to BE, and what is it that you desire to DO?

You have a Soul purpose and a Life purpose. You also can break down your purpose into subcategories, meaning you may have a different purpose within the larger purpose at each stage of your life.

But the overall theme of a life is the mission.

For instance, a mission could be assisting the awakening of humanity. Or to be a warrior for those who cannot fight for themselves.

So, along the journey of fulfilling our mission and living our purpose, we may find ourselves with all sorts of challenges. Some large, some small. Times when everything is flowing with ease and other times when everything seems to be difficult, falling apart, or chaotic.

What is happening when all seems to be challenging or chaotic?

These are the Dissolution points or the falling away of what no longer serves.

What is happening when there is a clearing of yourself and life?

These are the Purification points, the preparation for a new life and self.

What is happening when all is exciting and passion is flowing?

These are the Rebirth points, the connecting points creating new life.

What is happening when all is peaceful and serene?

These are the Living Union points when you have reached a new level of awareness and consciousness.

You can draw parallels to the primal forces of creation discussed earlier—the Three Gunas: Tamas, Rajas, and Sattva. Additionally, much like the stages of Alchemy we've delved into here—Nigredo, Rubedo, Albedo—similar connections can be made.

So the Divine truth in any stage is to be present in the moment. Offer up, according to your unique design, the energy that is best suited for you.

If you are in a **Nigredo/Tamas stage,** things need to deconstruct. There is a higher wisdom breaking apart things so something new can be created. This can present with intense fear and all sorts of emotions that seem to come from the darkest place. You can literally see blackness, decay, and death around you: the end to relationships, projects, a way of being, or even life. Physical pain can manifest here on all levels. It can be a complete and utter deconstruction of a part of your life. A clearing or reset is needed, or a change of path is coming in. Wisdom is attained here. This is the Yin phase.

If you are in a **Rubedo/Rajas stage,** things are in motion, movement is lining up points that will create connections and circumstances that are bringing in new opportunities. In the alchemical stage, this is the success of the Great Work. In creation, this can be the movement of all the new growth. There is passion and bliss here.

If you are in an **Albedo/Sattva stage,** things need to be still in the sense that you are clearing out and making new space. Rejuvenate now. This doesn't mean nothing is happening—this is the state where purging or cleansing can happen, reaching into pure states of peace. But, ultimately, what is happening is the "purest" form of transformation. This is the Yang phase.

When is it time to surrender, and when is it time to act or intend? This is related to the stage of creation that is before you. Check in with this.

Consider the Nigredo/Tamas/Dissolution phase as the ground, the foundation dismantling, followed by the revitalizing breath of fresh energy in the Albedo/Sattva/Purification stage. The subsequent rebuilding process can be likened to the Rubedo/Rajas/Rebirth phase.

When should we embrace surrender, allowing ourselves to be dormant and receptive, patiently awaiting? And when is it the right time to exert energy, take action, or extend a current?

How do you best "use" your energy? It is all in what is being mirrored to you within the stage.

Envision yourself as the culmination of all actions, exercises, activities, and intentions you've undertaken or established.

Reflect on the moments when you recognized, "I know what I need to do"—to heal, clear, resolve, transform, transmute, or let go of various aspects.

Consider every piece of energy you invested in attempting to alter things.

Now, release them all—every facet from this lifetime and others—into the transformative fire. Picture every instance when you sat in disconnect or despair, declaring, "Here is another piece I'd like to change."

I say now, lay them here. Lay them all here.

All the wounds, pain, disappointments, agonies, and all the connections to everyone connected to these "past" experiences, let them be here now.

I invoke the power of the Divine Presence to be the container for all of these offerings.

For now, that is what they are: offerings. Because when you surrender holding on to them, movement creates an effect of infinite proportions beyond what you can even comprehend.

You are AWAKENED.

You have remembered that you have it, have always had it, no one else had it, no one else gave it to you, and no place outside held it.

Presence is you in your alignment, and now we dive into the integrity of this.

Today, you push through that fear and realize it was just a veil you were meant to lift!

To assist you in staying in your true energy and on your Soul Path, here are some suggestions:

Sleep as much as you can. You are a newborn baby, newly born into this level you have arrived at. Also, sleep will be where your physical body can catch up to the energy body.

Give your body the nourishment it is asking for. Your physical body is now vibrating at a different frequency. Your cravings and tastes could be different.

Watch what you talk about/don't talk about. It may be different topics than usual, there may also be more silence and it is good to not share too much of your experience or process. Keep these details close to you. Keep their potency. The magic that happened to you may not be understood by many. It is precious to YOU. You can share the overall changes and your general experience, but just be mindful of the sacredness of your journey. And because what we think, say, and do now is only increasing in potency.

Watch what you give your time and energy to. In the past, you may have given attention to something because you thought it was important to do so. But you now realize that so much of what we are programmed to care about, even in the so-called "conscious" circles, is still just illusion, distraction, lies, and conditioning. PAY ATTENTION. In many ways there can be the sense that doing nothing and being quiet and still is more important than before.

Ask yourself: What do I REALLY want? This question is for the new version of yourself. Don't be surprised if your answer is very different than a month ago. Going forward, when creating anything, you must be very clear about what energy point you are operating from. Because you will create more easily, choose wisely. Continually discern what you truly want because who you were in that last moment is a totally different you than this moment. Be okay with a new you unfolding.

What does all this mean for you? It means you are stepping into your birthright to live as a Sovereign being.

Look at your life, every aspect, and start to see where you are still compromising this concept because you don't believe, trust, or truly feel it.

And then start to challenge yourself to do your daily routine, work, or "yourself" differently. Give up something you believe is part of your identity or a habit and change it. Allow for new grooves to create a new version of you.

Consider rereading this book every year. For every year, you are made anew. Every cycle, you are moving through a similar process, just with a new issue, person, or situation.

And every cycle has new discoveries.

You take the journey not for the destination, but for all the magic you experience along the way.

For what is life truly but the magic at the center of all things?

And discovering that the magic was always YOU.

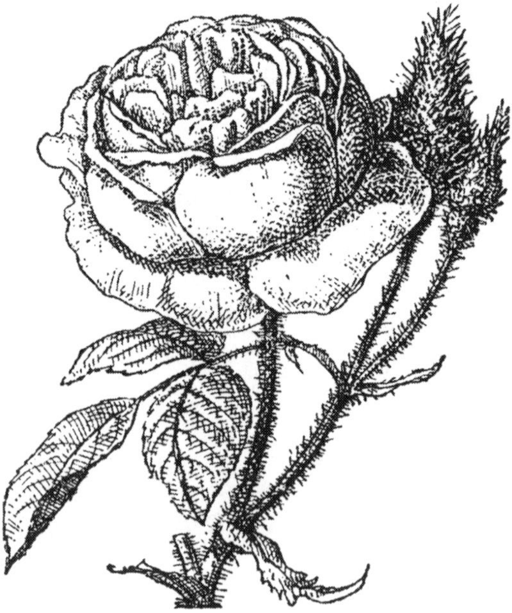

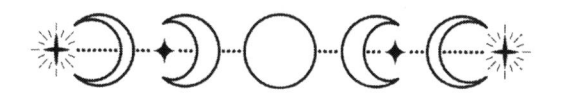

I AM

I AM the Yin and the Yang,
The male and the female,
The dark and the light,
Sacred Feminine and Masculine,
The red and the white.

I AM the Alchemical Union,
Body and Soul,
Shadow and bright.

I AM all That IS.

I AM the day and the night.
the left and the right,
the weakness and the might.

I AM THIS I AM
In all the blindness and the sight.

—Sarah Michelle Wergin

Acknowledgments

The creation of this book is due to so many beautiful souls who have inspired and supported me.

To my Mother, thank you for always believing in me; every unusual perspective, uncommon idea, otherworldly insight and wild understanding. You always understood me.

To my Father, thank you for all the support, encouragement, and unwavering dedication to help me see the next steps. Raja thanks you, too ;-)

To Auntie G, thank you for being my fairy godmother and earth angel as I followed this unknown path, and for reminding me that we are all cut from Divine cloth.

To Ani, for being the guide who helped me to awaken to my most precious memories that called in my own remembering.

To Jamie, for walking so many paths with me as I awakened to this material and to my own Divine Union—always being there to share midnight revelations or holding space while I shed yet another layer of self.

To Rosaria, for being that unwavering sister in the midst of the flame and fire.

To Florencia, for understanding me and this journey as if it was your own.

To Alicia, for all the guidance through this "land" of authoring.

To Eduardo, for being a gift of intense inspiration, revealing so many truths of Divine Union.

To Astara, my publisher, for believing in my work, vision, and message.

To Brooke, for being the light and beauty I needed so I could see what was possible.

To Aimee—I prayed for you and you arrived...there are no words to express my gratitude to you for helping me achieve this dream. Thank you for all your devotion, deep appreciation of this work and holding the vision of its importance...it is your talent that made this a reality. You being there to hold my hand as the creation manifested made all the difference.

To Raja, my beloved angel boy, thank you for being by my side through every moment, for doing the best job of "holding space" for me and each new chapter, for wiping my tears, making me laugh, taking me into the forest, and showing me how to run like the wind...you are my heart. Thank you for giving me the gift of being your momma. Together forever.

Resources

Alchemical Transformation Products

Awaken Alchemy Collection, www.awakeningdivineunion.com

Awaken: Sacred Anointing Oil, Mystical Crystal Elixir, Cleansing Aura/Space Spray, Embodying Tea and Invoking Incense

Crystals

AhhhMuse, www.ahhhmuse.com—use CODE 1280 to get 10% off!

Marilyn and Tohmas Twintrees—Crystal communicators and sellers, with the highest ethics of listening, caring and sharing love and light.

Flower Essences

Flower Essence Services, www.fesflowers.com

Flower Essences Bridging Body & Soul

Hatha Yoga/Yoga Nidra/Breathwork/Heart-Brain Coherence

Tend Conscious Wellness, www.tendmindbody.com, Online and in-person

Brooke Magnaghi is a HeartMath Mentor, and Yoga & Fitness Instructor working with private clients, corporations and small businesses to help individuals and staff reduce stress, stay fit, and cultivate resilience and self-awareness in body and mind.

Conscious Style-Brand Coaching

The Oracle of Style, www.rosariameek.com

Dr. Rosaria Meek, founder of Style coaching and executive presence training- Empowering your essence and elevating your confidence with style.

Hellenistic Astrology

Courtney Sanborn, www.courtneysanborn.com/astrology

Courtney has been immersed in astrology for close to 30 years. She practices Hellenistic astrology, the mystical tradition of horoscopic astrology that has been practiced since the first century.

"My use of Astrology is in service to helping you discover your deepest truth and expressing it through this life."

About the Author

Sarah Michelle Wergin, RN, LAc is a healer, priestess, and educator. As the visionary behind the Kwan Yin Clinic, a holistic healing center, and the Awakening Divine Union Mystery School, she guides individuals on the journey of self-discovery by harmonizing the body, mind, and soul with the Universal Oneness. Renowned for her insightful intuition, compassionate demeanor, and profound spiritual foundation, Sarah is a highly sought-after consultant. Her life's mission revolves around aiding each soul in recognizing their inherent power and unlocking their natural abilities to heal, create, and undergo transformation. A compelling speaker, Sarah exudes a serene, loving, and authentic presence, encouraging others to explore their personal power and embrace their authentic truth. With over 30 years of experience, Sarah Michelle Wergin has delved into numerous healing arts and spiritual traditions. She holds certifications/licenses as a Registered Nurse, Licensed Acupuncturist, Classical Feng Shui Practitioner, Functional Medicine Practitioner, Acutonics Sound Healer as well as many others. When not engaged with clients, Sarah immerses herself in ceremonial practices, enjoys the company of her furry companions, and seeks solace in nature, connecting deeply with Mother Earth.

Offerings

Awakening Divine Union 1:1 Alchemical Support—*Virtual sessions*

Open to receive what your heart and soul need. Let Sarah be your personal guide to transforming your life with the ancient tools, wisdom, and knowledge of Avalon, Ancient Egypt, Atlantis, Lemuria, and beyond.

Customized Healing-Teaching-Oracle just for YOU including:

+ Spiritual Path Alignment: mentoring/coaching/guidance to assist you in finding your mission and living your purpose
+ Physical Body: harmonizing any imbalances
+ Mental Body: fine tuning and repatterning your thoughts
+ Emotional Body: healing/clearing old traumas, wounds, and blockages

Health Consultations: Kwan Yin Clinic—*Virtual & in-person in Colorado & North Carolina*

Traditional Chinese Medicine, Western & Eastern Herbal Medicine, Functional Medicine & Sound Healing

Akashic Records Healing—*Virtual sessions*

The Akashic Records are the energetic library of everything that has been, is, and shall be. These records hold keys to assist your healing and evolution. Sarah Michelle Wergin is initiated to open the records for individuals. One enters the records to receive guidance and healing for transformation of the Soul.

Classical Feng Shui—*Virtual or in-person*

Classical Feng Shui is a complex body of knowledge that reveals how to balance the energies of any physical space to assure the health, peace, and good fortune for the people inhabiting it. Sarah Michelle Wergin blends her knowledge of Eastern Medicine and Feng Shui to bring you a unique and complete look at what is going on in your body, home, and business. Her combined approach to address where your imbalances are in all of these areas leads to a holistic treatment that re-establishes harmony and balance in every area of your life.

Sacred Retreats—*Virtual or in-person*

Take dedicated time with Sarah Michelle Wergin to step aside from your daily routine and be held in the sanctuary of the womb of the Divine while you deepen the experience of your awakening in the sacred temple.

Sacred Journeys: England—*In-person, small group travel*

We are being called to remember our ancient wisdom, reclaim our lost gifts, and rebirth our lives in Divine Purpose. Journey with Sarah through the sacred lands and return to Avalon. Travel along the Path of the Dragon, feel Mother Earth's currents, and merge with Her to activate your long-lost memories and forgotten power. This journey is not your usual tour of a distant land but one of pilgrimage, taking time at these sacred places for quiet reflection, meditation, and listening. Many ceremonies are offered along the way to assist each person's opening, remembering, and awakening.

Learn more about these and other offerings at **awakeningdivineunion.com**.

Visit us at www.floweroflifepress.com

Made in the USA
Middletown, DE
16 February 2024